THE WEB DESIGNER'S ROADMAP

The Web Designer's Roadmap

by Giovanni DiFeterici

Copyright © 2012 SitePoint Pty. Ltd.

Product Manager: Simon Mackie   **Editor**: Kelly Steele

Technical Editor: Diana MacDonald   **Cover Designer**: Alex Walker

Indexer: Michele Combs

Printing History:

   1st edition: August 2012

Notice of Rights

Notice of Liability

Trademark Notice

✦ sitepoint

Published by SitePoint Pty. Ltd.

48 Cambridge Street Collingwood
VIC Australia 3066
Web: www.sitepoint.com
Email: business@sitepoint.com

ISBN 978-0-9872478-4-1 (print)

ISBN 978-0-9872478-5-8 (ebook)
Printed and bound in the United States of America

About Giovanni DiFeterici

Giovanni is an illustrator, designer, and front-end developer at Period Three (http://www.period-three.com/), a web design firm in South Carolina. He's also the content and style editor for Unmatched Style (http://unmatchedstyle.com/), a design gallery and blog dedicated to documenting and curating all things both *badass* and web design-related. Giovanni regularly speaks at conferences about creativity, interface design, and art. Before becoming a designer, he was a fine artist for many years, which continues to inform his web design process and aesthetic. In addition, Giovanni's favorite comic book is Akira, he is the proud owner of a large red mohawk, and he believes Francis Bacon is the greatest painter ever.

About SitePoint

SitePoint specializes in publishing practical, rewarding, and approachable content for web professionals. Visit http://www.sitepoint.com/ to access our books, blogs, newsletters, articles, and community forums.

Table of Contents

Chapter 4   Form and Function

Chapter 5   Design Patterns: Tried and Trusted Solutions

Chapter 6   Conceptual Design and Our Color Project .. 117

Chapter 7   Designing in the Wild 153

Preface

Welcome to another book about web design! Well, actually, this one's different. This book will also delve into the creative side of designing for the Web, including a look at art history and some sources of inspiration for the intrepid web designer. In the main, we'll be discussing the phases of the design process and how to incorporate them into your workflow.

Some of these stages are tried-and-true, industry-strength sweet magic that the majority of designers use, even if they fail to realize it. We'll talk about these stages in great detail because they're going to be your bread and butter as a web designer. Much of what a web designer does is industry-specific and requires a great deal of technical knowledge (so you'll need to know some HTML), but the process is far more important as the vehicle that allows us to complete complex tasks without pulling out our hair.

Each step of the design process laid out in this book is something that you can adopt, change, or ignore. I personally believe that designers should work in whatever way best suits their skills. Some prefer to work in the browser with HTML and CSS. Others use Fireworks and create their wireframes and designs in the same project document. Some designers sketch thumbnails, while others don't.

I want you to be able to communicate your ideas, so that you can interact effectively with clients and the rest of your team. What I don't want is for you to treat this book as a step-by-step guide for how to be an "awesome-sauce" designer. You already have the awesome sauce. I'm just here to talk about the details.

I hope you enjoy the book, that you learn something new, and that you continue to grow as a designer. Many people have helped me reach this point. My only desire is to give something back.

Who Should Read This Book

This book is for web designers who seek a structured way to be creative when designing websites. It's ideal for designers who are just starting out, but is also useful for anyone looking for a different perspective.

Furthermore, if you've found yourself in any one of these scenarios, this book is for you:

- You're stuck on a design.
- You've been misinterpreting a client's needs.
- You want to learn some new techniques that all the cool kids are into.
- You've never considered your design process before, but want to get a handle on it.

If you picked up this book, chances are that you're curious about what you could change in your design process, and how to handle such change. So, this one's for you.

What's in This Book

This book comprises the following seven chapters.

Chapter 1: *Beauty, Creativity, and Inspiration*

By way of an introduction, I'll explain the book's broader concepts and establish the general terminology we'll be using. The book's ongoing project, Spectrumagic, is presented, where I'll set expectations about what you'll be learning. We'll also look at the relevance of the study of aesthetics, creative processes, and where to find inspiration.

Chapter 2: *It Ain't Over Till It's Over: A Bit of Design History*

Here, I'll present a brief history of design and show how the design process has changed over the years. In particular, I'll focus on the Modernist and Postmodernist eras to provide a context for the chapters that follow, as well as lay the groundwork for common design patterns.

Chapter 3: *Gathering Resources: That Rucksack Has a Lot of Pockets*

This chapter covers some practical lessons when deciding on the look of your design. It will include the discovery process, which involves learning from other disciplines, and resource gathering, which encompasses mood boards, color palettes, and storyboards.

Chapter 4: *Form and Function*

Now we'll learn about assessing the structural and technical needs of a website and its design. We'll look at the design's purpose, and how to best communicate interaction and hierarchy. Areas covered are designing for multiple form factors including mobile sites, responsive design, wireframes, strategy, and content grayboxing.

Chapter 5: *Design Patterns: Tried and Trusted Solutions*

Programming design patterns are proven solutions to problems that arise while developing applications. Web design also has its share of issues. In this chapter, we'll look at the most common design patterns, and possible use cases for when and how they should be implemented.

Chapter 6: *Conceptual Design and Our Color Project*

First, we'll address conceptual design and how we arrive at a theme that informs the design process. We'll look at a real-life example and cover topics such as designing the interface, art direction, and creative association. Then, we'll delve into our Spectrumagic project, implementing what we've learned. Along the way, we'll introduce the modern marvel that is style tiles and the notion of intuitive design.

Chapter 7: *Designing in the Wild*

Understanding the limitations of web-based technologies and how to overcome them is a necessary part of implementing designs. Often, a little knowledge ahead of time can help to shape a design and make front-end development easier. We'll also examine progressive enhancement and look at some fancy tools and apps that should make your designing life easier.

Where to Find Help

Design is an evolving subject, so chances are good that by the time you read this, some minor detail or other of these technologies has changed from what's described in this book. Thankfully, SitePoint has a thriving community of designers ready and waiting to help you out if you run into trouble, and we also maintain a list of known errata for this book you can consult for the latest updates.

The SitePoint Forums

The SitePoint Forums[1] are discussion forums where you can ask questions about anything related to web development. You may, of course, answer questions, too. That's how a discussion forum site works—some people ask, some people answer and most people do a bit of both. Sharing your knowledge benefits others and strengthens the community. A lot of fun and experienced web designers and developers hang out there. It's a good way to learn new stuff, have questions answered in a hurry, and just have fun. In particular, check out the design thread.

The Book's Website

Located at http://www.sitepoint.com/books/process1/, the website that supports this book will give you access to the following facilities:

Video Interviews

As you progress through this book, you'll note a number of quotes from interviews. See the book's website to see these interviews in full.

Updates and Errata

No book is perfect, and we expect that alert readers will be able to spot at least one or two mistakes before the end of this one. The Errata page on the book's website will always have the latest information about known typographical and code errors.

The SitePoint Newsletters

In addition to books like this one, SitePoint publishes free email newsletters such as the *SitePoint* newsletter, *PHPMaster*, *CloudSpring*, *RubySource*, *DesignFestival*, and *BuildMobile*. In them you'll read about the latest news, product releases, trends, tips, and techniques for all aspects of web development. Sign up to one or more of these newsletters at http://www.sitepoint.com/newsletter/.

Your Feedback

If you're unable to find an answer through the forums, or if you wish to contact us for any other reason, the best place to write is books@sitepoint.com. We have a well-staffed email support system

---

[1] http://www.sitepoint.com/forums/

set up to track your inquiries, and if our support team members are unable to answer your question, they'll send it straight to us. Suggestions for improvements, as well as notices of any mistakes you may find, are especially welcome.

Acknowledgments

I want to thank all the folks who contributed their time and words to this book. Here be titans!

Dr. Donald Norman (http://www.jnd.org/) is an industry legend in the field of user-centered design. His books and words have influenced generations of UX designers. I can't say enough about Don. He is amazingly intelligent and insightful in his evaluation of what it really means to be a designer. His ideas about product design and user experience are way beyond what most designers know. I can't thank him enough for giving me two hours of his life.

Meagan Fisher (http://owltastic.com/) is a wonderful designer with a lavish and beautiful style. I love her work and have nothing but respect for her. Meagan went into great detail about her process and how she interacts with clients, so you'll see her quotes all over the place.

Dan Rubin (http://about.me/danrubin) is a candid and thoughtful designer. I found my discussion with Dan to be amazingly thought-provoking. His mix of strong opinions and flexibility was refreshing, and helped me to see a variety of approaches that can lead to great design.

Dave Rupert (http://daverupert.com/) makes the "tiny jQueries." He and his ilk at Paravel are the minds behind http://themanyfacesof.com, **lettering.js**, **fittext.js**, and many other sweet little web designer treats. He's also funny as hell.

Sarah Parmenter (http://www.sazzy.co.uk/) has been running her own design shop for ten years, where she has made a major impression on the niche market of iOS design. She has a wealth of experience and was incredibly candid with me about her process, its shortcomings, and the changes she's made to be a better designer.

Shaun Inman (http://shauninman.com/pendium/) is a man apart. After working in the web industry and creating his own startup, Shaun decided to dedicate himself to game design, where he has authored a number of great casual games for iOS and desktop. He has a solid style and singular approach that I don't think I could match on my best day.

Daniel Burka (http://www.deltatangobravo.com/) is a man possessed. He's all over the map: Digg, Glitch, Milk, and now Google. I have nothing but respect for his quiet and thoughtful approach to the craft of design. More than any other person I've interviewed, Daniel has had the greatest effect on how I think about what I do. Thanks and good luck in all your present and future ventures!

Jessica Hische (http://jessicahische.is/) is an amazing lettering artist working out of San Francisco. She's worked with some incredible clients, and has a unique approach to her work and business that have made her an excellent influence on the industry.

Samantha Warren (http://badassideas.com/) is the lovely person behind Style Tiles. She unveiled this marvel of modern web design while I was writing this book, so I was unable to cover it in as much depth as I'd have liked. She has made a major contribution to web design with her approach to system design. The Twitter monster has just bitten Samantha, but I hope she'll still have time for the rest of us!

Gene Crawford (unmatchedstyle.com) is my homie. Gene and I have worked together for the last three years and have done some great things together. He's a true friend and listened to all my ideas and gripes while writing this book. He is my mentor, my partner, and my friend.

Jay Barry (http://petridisc.com/) taught me everything I know. Jay has been my art director for the last few years and is the third arm on the strange monster that is Period Three. He taught me web design, HTML, CSS, JavaScript, and a smattering of PHP. He's opinionated, gruff, and good-hearted. I hope he knows how much I appreciate his leadership and tutelage.

Conventions Used in This Book

You'll notice that we've used certain typographic and layout styles throughout this book to signify different types of information. Look out for the following items.

Tips, Notes, and Warnings

Hey, You!

Tips will give you helpful little pointers.

Ahem, Excuse Me ...

Notes are useful asides that are related—but not critical—to the topic at hand. Think of them as extra tidbits of information.

Make Sure You Always ...

... pay attention to these important points.

Watch Out!

Warnings will highlight any gotchas that are likely to trip you up along the way.

Chapter 1

Beauty, Creativity, and Inspiration

Every journey begins with a first step. In this book, we're going to talk about creativity and design. I'll paint a picture of how you can improve your designs by evaluating every stage of the production pipeline. As designers, it's important to understand the design process so that we can better control our end results.

This begs the question: What are we controlling? I'd say that we're trying to control the perceptions of our users. We want them to connect with our designs emotionally, to find an aspect of our designs worth admiring and liking. We want them to have the motivation and inclination to explore our designs and discover everything that they have to offer. We want them to love our designs.

To achieve this, we have to understand how users actually perceive designs. By learning about the design elements and user perceptions that we're attempting to control, we're more likely to invent creative designs that speak to our users and solve our clients' problems. This is the first step on our journey. In this chapter, we'll discuss beauty, creativity, and inspiration. My intention is to make these concepts easier to grasp while laying out some simple strategies for applying them to the design process. We'll also look at the design project we'll be creating together throughout the book.

Aesthetics: It's More than a Pretty Picture

"Beauty is rare in all nature's works, and in all works of art."

—Voltaire

Okay, so Voltaire takes a fairly bleak view on the existence of beauty—but you have to admit, he has a point. I mean, how many truly gorgeous things have you come across over your lifetime? And of them, how many are the result of human activity? Lots of things are pretty or impressive, but that's not the same as true beauty. Still, I'm less convinced that beauty is *rare*; perhaps it just takes a keen eye to see it. So let's be a little more positive and aim to find all the diamonds in the rough.

Aesthetics is the study of beauty in all its forms. As you can see in Figure 1.1, "beauty" can be applied to many areas: everything from garden flowers to mathematics. But while different items can be perceived as beautiful for various reasons, there's a link between the perception of beauty and our reasons for feeling connected to it. Most people would agree on the beauty of a starry night sky. And it's hard not to be in awe of the vast expanse that is the Grand Canyon. I live in South Carolina, which has lovely mountains. Sometimes, those massive slabs of granite look like mirrors when the sun hits them at the right angle. Magnificent.

Figure 1.1. Aesthetics can incorporate everything from culture, fashion, and education to personal experience

Often, we're unsure *why* it is we find these objects beautiful. Why is the Grand Canyon awe-inspiring? Why do some people get all choked up by a sunset? Why are we floored by some designs and not by others? What's the difference between pretty and beautiful, or good and great? It's safe to say we all want to make designs that are intuitive and encourage interaction, but what is intuition and how do we foster it for our target audience? We want our designs to be creative and inspiring, but what makes a design creative? And if a design is creative, does it naturally follow that it's inspiring? How do we shape a user's initial reaction to our design and generate the interest and trust that will make them want to use our site?

We'll cover this shortly.

First, we need to try to understand perception. Too often we seek the quick answer to everything. Quick solutions fail to promote understanding, which is what's needed to form your own answers.

A deeper understanding of any subject is helpful. When I first started working as a front-end developer, I knew very little about JavaScript. All I could do to power complex interactions in my applications was to implement other developers' jQuery plugins. After months of being frustrated by my inability to make significant changes to those plugins, I took the plunge and really learned about JavaScript. Now, not only do I edit plugins, I write my own. I truly understand what I'm looking at when I write and read JavaScript.

Perhaps many of you have had similar experiences. Eventually, most of us reach a point in our careers where we want a deeper understanding of why and how we perform tasks. It's more than just knowing what the best practices are; it's about *why* they exist. For design, that means learning about the theory and process of design. Voltaire may have seen little beauty in the world, but we know better. A keen eye and an informed mind can find all the beauty that the world has to offer. And if we're unable to find beauty, we can create it ourselves.

What is beauty?

Beauty is mostly subjective, so it's hard to define accurately and objectively. *The Oxford English Dictionary* has a fairly good definition of beauty: "a combination of qualities, such as shape, color, or form, that pleases the aesthetic senses, especially the sight."[1] Really, this is fancy talk for saying something looks good, but it still stops short of identifying the actual characteristics that result in "beauty."

Traditionally, qualities like symmetry and harmony are cited as in the formation of beauty, and certain proportions do seem to effect a pleasing shape. Pythagoras' **golden ratio** is the mathematical example often cited to formulate an object of beautiful proportions. Numerically, the golden ratio is 1 : 1.61803398874989 … (a recurring number), and it works like this: if a rectangle is formed using this ratio, where x=1 and y=1.61803398874989 … , and a square is placed inside the rectangle, the left-over rectangle's measurements are set to the golden ratio, as illustrated in Figure 1.2.

---

[1] http://oxforddictionaries.com/definition/beauty?q=beauty

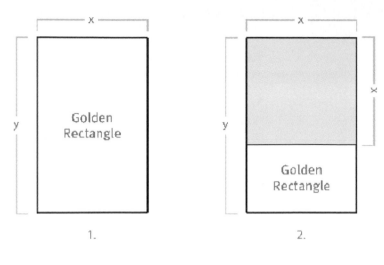

$$1 : 1.6180339887\ldots$$

Figure 1.2. Placing a square in a golden ratio rectangle creates another golden ratio rectangle

This offsetting of squares within the so-called "golden rectangle" can go on forever, the result of which is a near-perfect logarithmic spiral, as seen in Figure 1.3. Very cool.

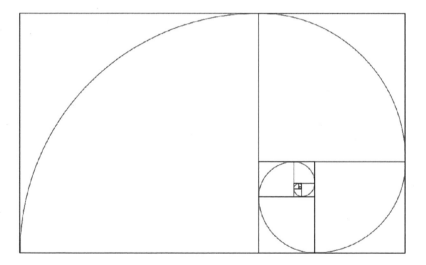

Figure 1.3. The golden ratio is considered inherently beautiful because of its apparent perfection

When I was taking figure-drawing classes in college, I was taught that the golden ratio can be frequently found in the human form. A perfectly proportioned face has many structures that can be measured with the golden ratio. Leonardo da Vinci's proportions for his famous Vitruvian Man—seen in Figure 1.4—are built around the golden ratio. Maybe that's why we find the ratio so compelling: it's a mathematical reflection of ourselves.

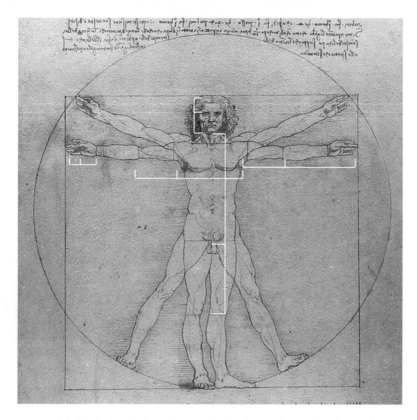

Figure 1.4. da Vinci's Vitruvian Man presents the golden ratio within the human form

The Eye of the Beholder

Let's face it, beauty is in the eye of the beholder, right? So, how do we reconcile our subjective impression of beauty with its objective qualities? Most of us can spy an object and think, "that's beautiful," but how many of us can give a purely objective reason why one item is beautiful and not another? We all have a unique view on what's beautiful, steeped in our individual opinions and perception. We're guided by our personal experiences, culture, and understanding of design.

Music is a good example for how culture and personal experience shape our opinions about beauty. Western music is based around a 12-tone musical system that, while versatile, has a particular character. Some Eastern music uses a completely different system with notes and patterns that may sound dissonant and off-putting to Westerners. That's not to say that one musical system is more beautiful than another; they just have different criteria for beauty.

Even within the same culture, beauty is subjective. Last year, on a cold winter morning, I took a picture of freshly fallen snow, seen in Figure 1.5. The morning was quiet and still, and no one had walked through the field across the street just yet. I wanted to capture the beauty of that moment, so I took a photo with my iPhone. Later, I showed the picture to a friend who missed the snowfall, and all he had to say was "bleak." Because he hadn't undergone the same experience, he was unable to see the reasons why I still found the image lovely. Instead of a serene moment, he saw a gray, lifeless scene.

Figure 1.5. Serene or lifeless, depending on your view

A Refined Sense of Beauty

There are designers who might believe they're more in tune with what looks good or is visually effective, as it's part of their job. Designers are certainly more familiar with the principles and elements of design, as most have had some formal design education and employ on a daily basis what they've learned. But that's not to say we have some innate sixth sense that allows us to assess beauty better than everyone else.

Most designers have an intuitive approach to their work. Over time, we've made assumptions about good design based upon our tastes and personal experiences. Trends also play a big role in design choices. As I'm writing this book, condensed typefaces, ribbon headers, and vintage textures are popular. But while they all generally look nice as Figure 1.6 shows, including any of these visual treatments in a design offers no certainty that a site will be effective or exceptional.

Figure 1.6. Following a trend is no guarantee of a good design

I've talked to many designers about how they go about their process, and the answers are mostly similar. With a little variance, designers fall into the same camp: they are "pixel pushers." It seems that most of us start our designs by slapping down a few elements and shifting them around. We build them slowly by responding to what feels right, working with little unexpected surprises that come out of intuitive exploration.

The design process is essentially trial and error—plus gut reaction. Sometimes, we're forced to work within the constraints of the project—such as brand guidelines, technical limitations, or client direction—but we tend to take a free hand with our designs. Eventually, the elements settle into place and a design is born. To a certain degree, we all employ this method. Most of the idea creation process is internal and unscripted. I'm sure that many intuitive designers start with wireframing and thumbnails—more on that in Chapter 4—but it's often quick and dirty. The amount of time allocated to the predesign phase is only a small part of the total process.

> "I generally start in Photoshop, just pushing pixels around and getting a feel for proportion and everything. I may chase down some dead ends and get stuck, and then I'll switch over to actual production, like exploring code and seeing what's possible. What I discover there will feed back into the design process and everything will start to inform everything else."
>
> —Shaun Inman

What's interesting about this approach is that it differs very little from what nondesigners do when they evaluate beauty. Gut reactions happen, by definition, unconsciously. The only real difference is that designers are trying to shape something that resembles beauty, while everyone else is trying to recognize it when they see it. But there's a problem in that purely intuitive design is mostly uncontrolled. Now, great work can come from a freewheeling process, but it has a tendency to keep us in our comfort zone and reinforce habits. We all do it. If we are short on time or have little to go on, the temptation is to pull something from our bag of tricks and slap a result together. This tends to happen because our process is so internal. And the more internal our design process, the more likely we are to put our designs on rails, forcing every project to accommodate our personal conventions.

 ## Know Your Audience

Sometimes it's okay to be completely subjective. When your audience's tastes closely resembles your own, appealing to their sensibilities can help you communicate more effectively. They'll appreciate your choice of imagery, language, and interaction between elements because their subjective experience closely resembles your own. Still, keep in mind that even great design—such as Figure 1.7—will fail if created for the wrong audience.

Figure 1.7. Designs that appeal to a narrow audience can be wonderful to some and off-putting to others

When most people think of the term "beauty," they're really thinking of "pretty." This conception of beauty emphasized in education, design, and art is easy to understand because it comes naturally. Our appreciation of beauty, for the most part, is innate. We see an object and we have feelings about it. It's natural and automatic. Culture and environment might change the criteria we use to evaluate beauty, but if it's there to see, we can't help but see it.

The seeing part is important. Most of our conscious and unconscious reactions to the world are a response to what we see. That our strongest sense of beauty should be created through vision, as represented in Figure 1.8, is a natural extension of how we perceive most things in the world around us.

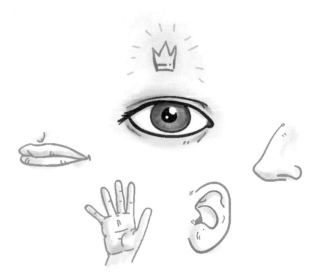

Figure 1.8. Beautiful objects may appeal to all the senses, but are primarily experienced through sight

Obviously, humanity's preoccupation with the way things look has a direct impact on all design. An object's looks can determine how we feel about it. Beauty is relevant not only because we desire to make items that are attractive, but because beauty has an immediate impact on users.

Perceived Beauty

Perceived beauty is the sense of beauty an observer feels in the first seconds of seeing an object. It's our snap judgment, before we've had a chance to really think about our opinions. **Perceived usability** is the impression a user has about how easy an app or site will be to use. It can vary greatly from one individual to another based upon their familiarity with similar interface designs, their confidence, and their personal tastes, among other factors.

Perception has a concrete role in communicating with an audience. Marketing specialists and user experience (UX) designers spend a great deal of time thinking about user perceptions because they want to exploit them. Marketers want to make their product desirable. UX designers try to make their product useful and intuitive. Most designers are taught that their job is to craft creative visuals for communication. To an extent, I agree with that job description, but I think it paints an incomplete picture. In addition, I'd venture that many designers want to make designs that are likable. Likability is a worthy goal, as evident in Figure 1.9, but interactive design is really a combination of all three goals: desirability, intuitiveness, and likability.

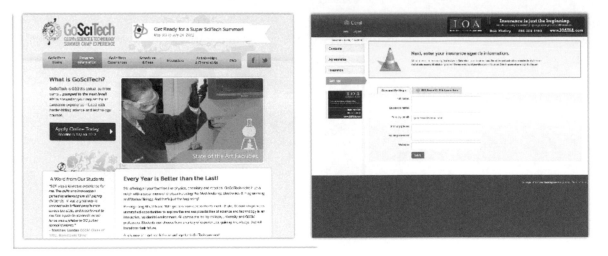

Figure 1.9. First impressions are important. Which of these two designs do you like and trust?

User experience expert Marc Hassenzahl conducted an interesting study to determine if there were any correlations between the perceived beauty of an interface and its perceived usability. In other words, did users think that good-looking designs worked better? During the study, he had users compare and contrast various skins for a desktop MP3 player. The results were revealing.

Basically, Hassenzahl found that users' first impressions of a design are greatly affected by whether or not they consider it beautiful. However, after users have poked around for a while and gotten a real taste of how everything works, their opinions become far less influenced by beauty. Once they've spent time with a design, perceived usability is mostly determined by ease of use. The condensed message is this: in the beginning, users like and trust designs that look good. In the end, they like and trust designs that work well.

 ## Consider Your Users' Uniqueness

Generalizing "users" to include every person who will ever look at your product is a bad idea, because every audience is different. Expectations about feature sets, complexity, and design sophistication can vary greatly depending on a user's level of expertise, but even savvy users will be frustrated by design choices that make incorrect assumptions about their habits. Clearly, if you're designing an application to be used primarily by other interactive designers, the criteria for quality will differ greatly from an application designed to educate children.

Understandably, most designers think primarily about surface beauty, especially web designers. Who can blame us? It's our job. We're all ad hoc UX designers, but mostly, we want our work to look good. A lot of us are without a background in UX; we're not engineers, and we don't do much research into user-centered or ecological design. And that's okay. Most of the time, the production pipeline prohibits us from branching out into other disciplines; we get siloed and spend the bulk of our time focused on visually skinning apps and websites.

But surface beauty is only part of the story. It really pays to explore outside of our industry. There are some really intelligent people leading the way in web design with great ideas and amazing talent, yet they're also apparent in other fields. Over the last few years, we've built an aesthetic that borrows heavily from art and design, but other influences exist as well. Even mathematicians have their own ideas about beauty. Let's now take a little detour and see how a mathematical sense of beauty is connected to interactive design.

The Elegance of Science

When I was a kid, I wanted to be a scientist. I read *A Brief History of Time* (New York: Random House, 1998),[2] in which Stephen Hawking gives a plain English explanation of cosmology. I also read Brian Greene's *Elegant Universe* (New York: WW Norton, 2003),[3] in addition to other layperson-style books on the subject. *Elegant Universe* is about string theory. While the maths is a bit beyond me (seriously, what's an eleven-dimensional universe?), I do understand that string theory is a good stab at creating one theory of physics that explains how the universe works.

What's always been most interesting to me is the idea that one theory should explain everything. Why have one theory for an entire universe? Why not two? I started exploring reasons why scientists thought there should only be one theory, and this led me to the idea of mathematical elegance.

From a mathematical perspective, **elegance** is the idea that a proof or equation should be succinct, economical, and irreducible. Einstein's equation $E=mc^2$ is an excellent example of this idea. $E=mc^2$ is read as: energy equals mass multiplied by the speed of light squared. This equation reveals that energy and mass are equivalent entities. At the time this equation was composed, mass and energy were considered to be completely different entities. $E=mc^2$ fundamentally changed the way physicists thought about the universe. The equation is elegant because it condenses a vast amount of information into a tiny statement.

What's interesting about this is that it's a completely different set of criteria for determining beauty. Elegance has nothing do with the way it looks and everything to do with the effectiveness and economy of the final result. The equation is beautiful because it accomplishes so much with so little. A wealth of information about how the universe is glued together is contained in five characters.

Upon thinking about the concept of mathematical elegance, it became clear to me that UX designers and physicists are trying to achieve the same kind of elegance. The aesthetics differ only in the detail. Physicists are trying to create succinct, powerful equations that explain as much as possible. UX designers are trying trying to create succinct, powerful experiences that communicate intent and action without confusing content. The goals for creating a great user experience are not necessarily about making it beautiful on the surface. UX design is about crafting intelligent and effective solutions for conveying interaction and organization, as Figure 1.10 indicates.

---

[2] http://www.randomhouse.com/book/77010/a-brief-history-of-time-by-stephen-hawking
[3] http://books.wwnorton.com/books/detail.aspx?ID=5682

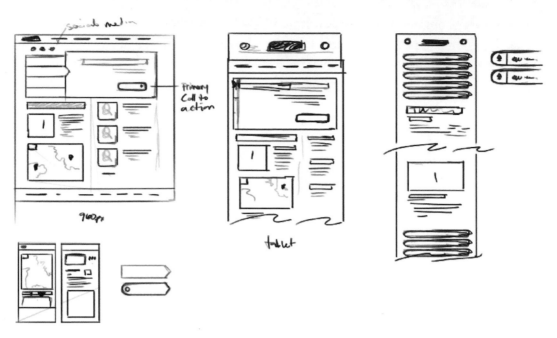

Figure 1.10. Good UX design is all about effectiveness and economy

By incorporating concepts like mathematical elegance into our design philosophy, we come to realize that design is about more than making a pretty picture. An emphasis on crafting economical and intuitive solutions can help us build designs that empower users to learn quickly and enjoy the experience of using our sites and applications. By considering elegance, we can apply our understanding of surface beauty to create a strong framework of interaction for designs that are both visually stunning and easy to use.

> "I think that there are people who are primarily visual designers and their major role is style and polish. You can hand something to them that is mostly [complete], and say, 'We need good iconography. Tie our brand to this page.'
>
> I think there is a role for people like that, but I'm much more interested in broader product design, where the designer helps establish the most fundamental product directions. Is this actually the right product for our business? Is our business doing the right thing? Are we selling the right widgets? Asking these questions is part of a designer's role."
>
> —Daniel Burka

Drawing a blank? Let's Look at Dribbble

> "Good artists borrow, great artists steal."
>
> —Pablo Picasso (allegedly)

Fine artists take this to be an explanation of the difference between artists who copy their peers and artists who assimilate the ideas of their peers. It's a clever quote, once you think it through: if you simply copy (borrow) ideas from other designers, they're doing all the work while you take some of the credit. But if you instead learn (steal) from another design, you've incorporated the ideas and grown as a designer. After all, we all build on the works of our predecessors to a degree. Taking cues from other designers is unavoidable, and with the number of websites out there growing by the thousands, truly original and innovative designs are becoming harder to create. Many designers struggle with creativity; fortunately, various online galleries (such as unmatchedstyle.com in Figure 1.11) curate some of the best websites around so that designers can find the inspiration they need.

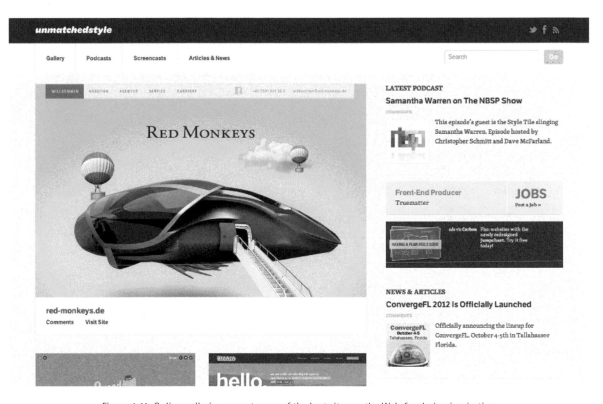

Figure 1.11. Online galleries present some of the best sites on the Web for design inspiration

Creativity is difficult to define, but I'd say it amounts primarily to a person's ability to make something that's novel and unexpected. Just about every site, article, or book about creativity that I've read offers a unique definition, but few diverge too far from that central idea. Creativity requires some level of decision-making. A sunset may be beautiful, but it's not creative; however, a painting or song about a sunset may be both. Creativity has a definite human element that makes it mysterious and compelling. Almost every industry admires and exploits creativity. Entire businesses and revolutions are built around the creative enterprises of one individual: think Steve Jobs (Apple) and Mark Zuckerberg (Facebook). Design is no different.

Creativity is essentially about composing new ideas. It may be a new twist on an old idea. It can be bold or subtle. Highly creative designs are admired, even when they break all the rules and defy convention, such as what's achieved by Ginger Whale[4] in Figure 1.12. It can also be off-putting and confusing.[5] Creativity can be any number of things, but it's always about finding something new. For instance, a web page featuring unconventional navigation combined with appealing illustrations and subtle animations, as in Figure 1.12, piques your interest, making you want to poke around and explore.

Figure 1.12. Unconventional navigation and cute illustrations engage with the user

For many designers, originality and creativity is a driving goal and central tenet of their practice, and they intentionally buck convention to explore every possibility. Other designers are more utilitarian and diverge less from standard industry practices and patterns. Both approaches to design can produce compelling and useful results, but often the creative solution is afforded more credit and praise. Why? Why should we quest for originality? Should novelty and independence be a goal?

Standing on the Shoulders of Giants

We all want to make our mark on the industry and have a style that sets us apart from other designers. Many designers find this difficult because they base their style on the work of designers that they respect or admire. To some degree we're all derivative in our choices, because our understanding of what is beautiful is a reaction to what we see. We build on the accomplishments of other designers; standing on the shoulders of giants, as the saying goes.

---

[4] http://gingerwhale.com/

[5] If you ever have the chance, take a look at the *Codex Seraphinianus* by Italian artist and author, Luigi Serafini (Milan: Ricci, 1981).

The problem comes when a designer adopts a style simply because it looks good, without understanding why a style or aesthetic is appropriate for a specific design. All designs should incorporate design patterns that are well understood by users and have a strong utilization of the principles and elements of design, as well as a singular approach to accomplishing the business goals of the design.

Great design isn't necessarily dependent upon how creative it is. It's about communicating a message and accomplishing goals. Even so, we honor creativity and try to become more creative by trying new tricks. What is often glossed over is the creative process. Over time, we all develop a process by which we generate ideas. Some of us sketch and some of us write on Post-it notes. Some of us just skim the CSS galleries and look for designs similar to the one we need to create. I like to write outlines to help me organize my thoughts and sketch thumbnails of design elements. I also employ conceptual design in most of my work (more on that in the section called "Conceptual Design: Just a Little Black Magic" in Chapter 6). Whatever the process, even if it's just to mull matters over in your mind for a while, everyone has one.

Creativity: Don't Think about Pink Elephants

Are you thinking about pink elephants?[6]

With some projects, the ideas seem to pop out of nowhere; we become energized and can't wait to tackle the task at hand. One idea seems to spawn another, until we're positively drowning in possibilities. Projects like that can be uplifting and inspire us to go the extra mile. We put in extra hours to help a design realize its true potential. At those times, design is fun and exhilarating, and we remember why we chose this profession.

Sadly, not every project is so rosy. Crafting new ideas can be hard. Projects can be daunting for a number of reasons. A lack of knowledge about a site's content can leave us with limited ideas about how to present it. Looming deadlines can hinder our ability to focus. More interesting projects can divide our attention and keep our thoughts elsewhere. A million and one things can interrupt the flow of creativity. So how do we overcome these problems?

In a word: structure.

Our thoughts are naturally nonlinear, so the creative process is unstructured. Our brains flit from thought to thought faster than we realize. Without a structured creative process, coming up with new ideas is mostly a jumbled mess of half thoughts, flashes of imagery, and overlapping priorities, as Figure 1.13 shows. Evaluating a dozen ideas simultaneously can be overwhelming, leading us to think that we lack good ideas because we reject them too quickly.

---

[6] http://en.wikipedia.org/wiki/Ironic_process_theory

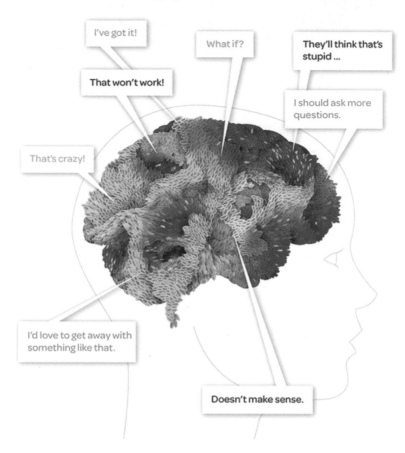

Figure 1.13. When our thoughts are a jumbled mess, it's hard to organize our ideas

We must avoid being too critical when we're trying to be creative. Come up with an idea, then move on to the next one. We can be critical later.

Adding Structure to the Creative Process

Following a structured set of steps can help us organize our thoughts and solidify ideas. It also allows the time and focus needed to give every idea a fair chance. Each idea has its merits and shortcomings. To overcome our natural tendencies, let's evaluate each stage of the creative process and propose a couple of strategies to keep us on track when we're coming up with new ideas.

 Understand the Problems You're Solving

I'm going to call this step zero because we need this before we even begin our creative process. We should never lose sight of the fact that all our creative ideas are in the service of our clients' needs. Your absolute first task should be to identify what problems you're solving. Only then can you shape great ideas that serve a direct purpose.

Most creative people have their own take on the process, but I try to keep it simple. I think of it in four stages:

Step 1: Brainstorming

Brainstorming is about coming up with ideas quickly and effortlessly. It's important that nothing be criticized during this phase. Every idea—no matter how wild or expensive or absurd—is on the table, without question. A brainstorming session should create an open environment where everyone can express themselves without judgment. You need to feel like any idea is worthwhile, even if it's likely to be axed later on.

It doesn't matter how you generate ideas; whatever works for you and your team is fine. What matters is that it should be fun, and no one feels pressured. If your team is competitive, make a game of it. Find a strategy that pits each person against each other and just have fun with it. If your team is less competitive, find a strategy that is more passive and collaborative.

Remember, you are just trying to encourage people to think laterally; you *want* them to be all over the place. I've found that having a really big whiteboard is key. Here are a couple of word exercises that have worked for me in the past to help you get the ball rolling.

Word Association

Whoever is at the whiteboard calls out words related to the project, and people in the group shout out whatever comes to mind, which is then recorded on the whiteboard. This creates a long list of word associations that can help direct new ideas. If you have a large team, breaking into small groups can be an excellent way of generating a hodgepodge of different ideas.

Clustering

Everybody writes down an important feature of the project on a note card. They may write project goals, ideas that should be conveyed, or emotions that the user should feel. Anything thought to be important goes on a card. For instance, if there are five people working together, each person writes down 10 points they believe to be important about the goal they're trying to accomplish. Then, all 50 cards (in this case) are laid out and "clustered" into closely related groups. This helps to organize all the project considerations, so that each goal is clearly defined and can be evaluated individually. Each cluster then becomes a new subject for brainstorming.

Step 2: Ideation

After your team—or just you, if you work alone—have brainstormed a number of ideas, some time can be spent riffing off each idea. Create variations on each theme. If you have too many ideas, just investigate the ones that resonate with people.

What's important about this stage is to see the flexibility of each idea. You want to know if an idea is fertile ground for more ideas. Can an idea be elaborated upon or changed for different circumstances? Consider everyone's reaction to each idea. If no one is excited about an idea or has anything to add, it might be an indication that the idea is a dud.

Step 3: Evaluation

During this phase of the creative process, ideas are given their first critical analysis. This is where people who are good at dissecting ideas thrive. Every idea should be put through its paces, and is either accepted as worthwhile, modified to be improved, or chucked out.

Saving critical analysis until the third phase is key. After ideas have been shuffled around long enough, they take on a life of their own, separate from the people who thought of them. It's far easier to dissect an idea if you're not having to worry about a colleague's feelings. This disassociation promotes honesty and constructive criticism while limiting confrontation. Look for the sweet spot between business considerations, creative ideas, and realistic implementation. As Figure 1.14 reveals, that's where the magic happens.

Figure 1.14. Where the magic is

Budgetary concerns, business goals, and considerations about audience should be considered in tandem with each idea. This is a great way to eliminate ideas that fail to solve the problems at hand as mentioned in the note Understand the Problems You're Solving. Every problem is connected to business goals that must be met. Only ideas with the potential to achieve those goals make it through the evaluation process.

I find it helps to have definite restrictions and criteria that can be applied to each idea. Make a list of all the project requirements and attack your laundry list of ideas with a hatchet. You want to separate the wheat from the chaff. Don't be afraid to cut the list of 50 ideas down to five or fewer. You're seeking the best of the best.

Beware of Vague Goals

If one of your goals is to "make something awesome" as in Figure 1.15, you might find that every idea satisfies that particular requirement. It's okay to have that as a goal, but it's not very specific. If all your goals are equally vague, you might need to go back and reevaluate what it is that you're trying to accomplish. If you're unable to address the problem clearly, you can't develop creative solutions to it.

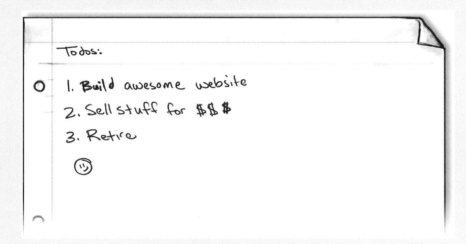

Figure 1.15. This outline is a little light on details

Step 4: Conversion

Eventually, you need to test your ideas. Hopefully, you've managed to hone your list of ideas to a couple of strong candidates. Take a little time to work up some preliminary sketches for the design. Produce a band of thumbnails and mock up some quick interface samples. This usually takes little time and can save your bacon later on. You want to avoid going too far down a road that isn't going to work out just because you wanted to bypass sketching a few thumbnails. Sometimes great ideas turn sour when put on paper. You need to take your ideas for a spin to see if they really make the cut.

Once you've undergone the creative process, you might find that there are gaps. No problem; go back to brainstorming and attack those new issues! These steps are designed to help you generate ideas and bounce them off each other. Don't be afraid to go at it a couple of times to get the best answers. Throw your ideas at as many people as you can find, in whichever way you choose, such as in Figure 1.16. Each person sees things slightly differently from the next, so let everyone participate in your brainstorming sessions. You never know who'll have that breakthrough idea.

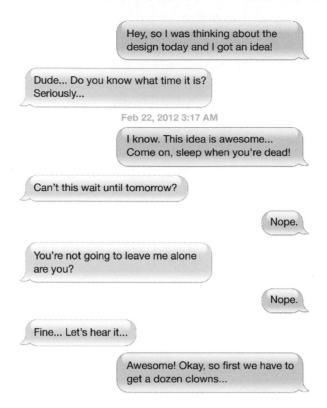

Figure 1.16. Bounce your ideas off friends and colleagues, no matter how inane it might sound at first

 Creativity Is Hard

Like anything worth knowing, creativity is a complex subject that is unable to be adequately explained in a few pages. Creativity is really a combination of inspiration, technical expertise, and experience. I don't advocate one creative process over another, but following these few steps has helped me develop ideas and solve problems that would have me come unstuck. What really matters is to find a way to excite your imagination and have fun.

The Disney Method

I learned about creativity and the creative process from my instructors in school. I attended Winthrop University and achieved a Fine Arts degree in Painting. While there, I learned about the so-called **Disney Method**. Whether or not this method was employed by its namesake exactly as I was told is irrelevant; it's a great way of thinking about how to compartmentalize the different phases of the creative process.

According to the theory, Walt Disney tried to foster the separate phases of the creative process by making them a concrete reality. The aim was to create environments that complemented each phase so that the creative team would think a certain way, depending on their location. See Figure 1.17 for a breakdown of the phases Disney used.

Figure 1.17. The Disney Method gets people in the right headspace to develop great ideas

Here's how it worked. Disney's creative team had three separate rooms dedicated to the development of new ideas. Each room represented a phase of the creative process and was designed to promote that phase and suppress the others.

The Dreaming Room

The first room was for the dreamer, so the creative team would go there to dream up new stories. Like our brainstorming sessions, every idea was valid and worthwhile in the dreaming room. It was a free and open space where people could let their imaginations run amuck. In the stories I've heard, chairs in the dreaming room were arranged in a circle as in Figure 1.18 so that everyone was engaged and involved.

Figure 1.18. Chairs are arranged in a circle to encourage free thought

The Realist Room

The second room was for the realist. In this room, the team would assess the practical applications of the new ideas. They'd evaluate the ideas dreamt up and decide what it would take to make them a reality. This is a slight departure from our creative process of brainstorming, ideation, and evaluation, but my guess is that the realist room was also where ideation occurred.

Again, the room was reputed to have a particular arrangement of chairs. In the realist room, the chairs were arranged in a semicircle in front of each idea, as in Figure 1.19. The arrangement was designed to promote some distance between the idea and the team debating its qualities. People could still freely discuss and collaborate on ideas, but the idea in question was given a little space.

Figure 1.19. Chairs are arranged in a semicircle to help focus on one idea at a time

The Critic Room

The third room was for the critic. In this room, ideas would be passed through the critical eye of the needle. The chairs were arranged in rows facing toward the idea in question, as in Figure 1.20. Instead of a shared experience, participants were isolated so that they evaluated the idea on their own.

Figure 1.20. Chairs are assembled theater-style to enable each person to be highly critical

Team members would judge the idea by trying to anticipate the problems it might create. They would measure it against past Disney projects and determine if it had true merit. Once an idea took a beating in this room, it would go back to the dreaming room and the process would start over (this is what's known as **iteration**). The cycle would be repeated until an idea reached the critic room and was met with total silence. If the critics had nothing to say, it meant the idea was ready for production. Silence would indicate that the idea was solid enough, because no reasonable criticism could be made of it.

To be frank, I'm unsure if the Disney Method was really implemented this way. I've always taken it to be an illustration of the different phases of the creative process and the need to keep them organized. No specific creative process is right or wrong. What's important is having a method that creates an environment where people can feel free to express their ideas and opinions. Anything that helps you generate ideas is well worth the effort.

Inspired By and Inspired To

In some ways, inspiration has a dual nature,[7] and separating these two kinds is essential to understanding our design motives.

On one hand, we can be galvanized *by* something. A song can be uplifting, where we're moved by its quality or message. Likewise, great design can motivate simply because we admire it. Seeing amazing work can energize us, making us feel good about our profession. This kind of stimulus is general and mostly undirected. Greatness and beauty can create feelings of awe that affect us emotionally. When we're inspired by something, we are identifying its admirable qualities and creating an emotional link to them. This state of inspiration is powerful and can create a sense of importance and wonder.

On the other hand, we can be inspired *to do* something. Once an object inspires us, we often seek to exemplify the qualities that we found influential. Witnessing the hard work and dedication of a co-worker might encourage us to act. Because these qualities are worth aspiring to, seeing a friend or colleague exhibit them can energize us to do the same.

Technological advancement also inspires people in our industry to innovate. Tools and techniques that make certain jobs easier have condensed production times and enabled us to be more progressive. For instance, dynamically updated charts and graphs in websites used to be difficult to create. Now, third-party plugins and progressive CSS3 allow us to create these kinds of visuals relatively simply. Even this one shift has allowed us to approach graphical information from a different angle. For a while the 960-grid system[8] was the baseline for most websites. 960 pixels was a good round number to work with and fit most browsers quite well. Now, smartphones, net books, and tablet computers have created a situation where a one-size-fits-all approach fails to cut it anymore. Websites have to be viewable across multiple platforms. Phones can be smaller than 400 pixels wide, while high-

---

[7] Thrash, T.M., *Journal of Personality and Social Psychology*, Vol. 87, No. 6, Dec. 2004, p. 958
[8] http://960.gs/

resolution monitors may exceed 2,000 pixels in width. This problem inspired the creation of re-sponsive design, where one CSS document can accommodate any form factor.

 Design Outside Your Comfort Zone

We tend to craft sites to our own taste, whether we realize it or not. We use imagery that speaks to our preferences and language that resonates with how we think. But don't be afraid to venture outside your comfort zone. If you find yourself dipping into the same well of ideas over and over again, it might indicate that you need to find new creative sources. Always be open to different ideas.

Clients can be a source of inspiration too. Most of the time, they know more about their audience than we do. They might not know the best way to communicate to their audience, but it's likely they'll be aware of details that we lack. If you're building a website for a company that manufactures golf clubs, but have never set foot on a green, it's likely that you have no understanding of the site's audience or the content. Clients have detailed knowledge of subjects we never think about. Talking to them can be great for getting the creative juices flowing. Have an open mind and they will often lead you to solutions and visuals that you'd never have thought of on your own; for instance, consider Figure 1.21. They can help you grow as a designer.

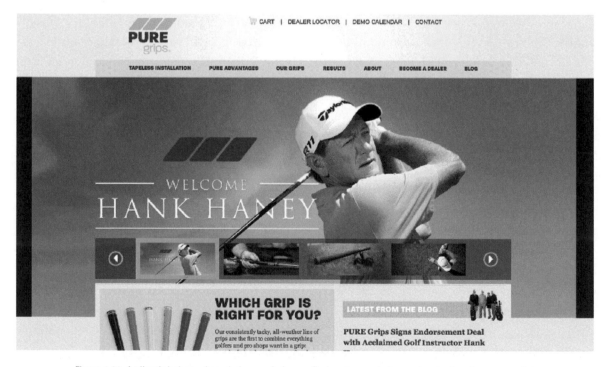

Figure 1.21. A client's industry knowledge can help you flesh out your design and make the site more useful

Involving the client also tends to keep them happier because they can see their own ideas integrated in the final product. They take some ownership for the design and are therefore more invested.

Design Galleries

Some of the greatest design on the Web pops up in online galleries every day. Architecture, vintage posters, nature, a new song on the radio, and so forth inspire us all the time. Technology and new-fangled tools inspire us to try new processes. I've been building responsive websites for over a year now but I didn't have any inclination to try `min-width` based media queries (more on that later!) until my art director built a great responsive site and I saw how much the approach cut down on redundancy in his CSS.

This kind of personal inspiration is reactionary; it exists in the moment and is unpredictable. It energizes us to be bold and try new things. It's also fickle. It can't be relied upon to help us solve concrete and unrelated problems on a daily basis. To find a more utilitarian kind of inspiration, we need to have some techniques for harnessing our curiosity.

Derivative Design: Copy cats or like minds?

We all go to CSS galleries to see what our heroes and competitors are up to. We want to see the next big design trends and keep pace with the breakneck pace of our industry. The blank white of the brand new Photoshop document can be daunting.

Having a massive collection of highly successful designs in one place is an amazing asset. The people who curate these galleries do so to document innovation and quality. When we see something that we like, we… ahem… "borrow" from it. Borrowing from the good decisions of great designers is a component of our industry, but we want to be ethical designers and blatantly stealing from the work of our peers is bad mojo. Taking a second to identify why we are inspired by a design we admire can help us to learn from great design without being unethical.

Keeping an Open Mind

What I love about design is that basically anything can be a source of inspiration. Lots of designers love comic books and vintage typography. We love old toys and photography. Letterpress is held dear by all, but anything can be a source of inspiration. I'm a painter who became a designer, so I draw a lot of my inspiration and ideas from that background. You may have completely different interests that appeal to you. Your interests and opinions are what differentiate you from others.

It's funny, but many of us have strong opinions on how to define "good design." The truth is that lots of designers are excellent at their craft. One aesthetic can differ from another—and they can both be right. There are no absolutes. A design that is perfect for one project could be absolute rubbish for another. You have to keep an open mind and look for the best parts of everything you see.

Developing Good Habits

Lots of us look for inspiration the same way every time. We go to galleries and look at other web design, but this can prevent us from breaking away from the strong influences of prominent and influential web designers who set the tone for our industry. I'm not against CSS galleries, but I'd encourage everyone to abandon this habit and start exploring design in all its forms. Look for inspiration in subjects and objects that have nothing to do with design. No design problem has one absolute solution. The broader your field of vision, the more options you create for yourself.

A little caveat about design galleries: studying the successful parts of great design can be a worthwhile learning experience, but I do think it pays to go outside your area of expertise and learn how other industries communicate. My understanding of the aesthetics of interaction came from reading a book about physics and applying the idea of mathematical elegance to the aesthetics of interaction design. Other disciplines have an entirely different approach to the way they solve problems. Learning from as many approaches as possible can do nothing but add to the industry. Ask yourself this question: If all I do is derive my designs from the successful work of other designers, have I really done anything?

Spectrumagic: Our Design Project

Throughout this book, we'll be using an ongoing project, Spectrumagic, to demonstrate the creative and design process. A sneak peek can be seen in Figure 1.22.

Figure 1.22. Fun with Spectrumagic

I'm going to outline the project here so that you, dear reader, have a clear understanding of the criteria. Think of this as the client's parameters. Imagine that you've taken on this project and the client has sent over a written description of what it wants:

- Spectrumagic is an educational site about color. It is a highly interactive and dynamic experience that teaches the reader about the science of visible color and the practical application of color theory.

- It is primarily designed for high-school students, but should be accessible to middle-school students and adults as well.

- It will work on tablet devices and all modern browsers. It will have a tactile feel that promotes interaction.

- It will include extensive content that is broken into two distinct categories: the science of color, and color theory. Each category will have a quiz that users can take to test their knowledge. Half the quiz will comprise multiple-choice questions, and the other half will be an interactive game.

- It will be highly visual and provide some kind of visual feedback about the user's progress through the content.

- It will incorporate the Spectrumagic brand.

Spectrumagic sounds like an interesting project and I hope it's already gotten your cogs moving. Think about the possibilities! The site revolves around color. It's for kids. It incorporates games with education. Spectrumagic has great potential for being an exciting and challenging project. Right now, the possibilities are wide open and we'll explore every detail of the project in due time.

Luckily, our client has provided some clear-cut requests and a simple branding document. Often, clients stop short of providing this level of guidance. If you find yourself faced with a project and no direction, do yourself a favor and talk to the client. Even a few sentences are better than nothing. You need something concrete to tell you where to start. Having clear direction makes composing a set of basic design requirements far easier.

Over the next six chapters, we'll explore every stage of the design process for Spectrumagic. We'll develop creative ideas for accomplishing our client's goals. We'll plan complex interactions, add game-like features to our site, and employ a feedback loop into our design. We'll develop a distinct visual language that helps our users to navigate pages and parse through information.

Finally, we will mock up a responsive design that accommodates mobile devices and tablets. Then we'll design each breakpoint (covered in the section called "Responsive Design" in Chapter 4) for our front-end developers to reference.

What have we learned?

In this chapter, we covered quite a bit of ground! We talked about the nature of beauty, creativity, and inspiration, and learned how to apply these concepts to our work, crafting great designs that satisfy our clients' needs and pique our users' interest.

We also laid out a creative process that we can utilize to help generate ideas and work collaboratively with our peers, all without losing sight of the practical problems that we're trying to address. Obviously, it's impossible to give the subject of creativity the attention it deserves in just one chapter, but I trust you've learned a little about what it means to be creative and how to capture and apply your ideas.

Finally, we addressed some rules of thumb that can help keep you on track in your projects:

- listen to clients; they know more than we think
- be ethical; learn from other designers and avoid ripping them off
- keep an open mind
- learn, learn, learn

In the next chapter, we'll talk a little about the history of design. This will give us a better understanding of our current design environment.

2

It Ain't Over Till It's Over: A Bit of Design History

I know what you're thinking: "Aargh! Don't bore me with history! I got enough of that in school." I can hardly blame you; I've never been a fan of memorizing lists of dates or the names of people long dead; it's hard enough remembering phone numbers. Still, knowledge of history benefits us by putting everything we do as designers into context.

Every day that we create design, we place ourselves into the timeline of art history. All the decisions that we make are colored by the work of our predecessors. We employ a set of principles and accept them as the norm. We take these principles to be self-evident, but that wasn't always the case.

Do you know that we design in an era of Postmodernism? You are almost certainly a postmodernist, whether you realize it or not. Were you aware that the design theory we apply has connections to philosophy, politics, and literature?

In 20 years, historians will look back at the advances we make and pass judgment. Whether we want it or not, we are merely a phase of a larger art timeline. Let's take a look at how we fit in.

Breaking the Cycle

Design is like high fashion. The trends are seasonal. Every year some new shiny style or cutting-edge technique makes a splash. Staying on the cutting edge is important in our industry.

When it comes to technology, your options are fairly cut and dried: either adopt the new technology or don't. Modernizr hits the scene; use it. JavaScript is supplanted by CoffeeScript; hit the books and embrace the meta in your programming. CSS selectors got you down? Switch to a precompiler, such as Sass or LESS. You can choose to follow the cool kids, or stick with the old guard.

Design is a little different. Tons of academic research is thrown at the problems of interaction and design, but we tend to favor anecdotal evidence and trial and error. We like to watch our heroes and learn from their experience. Most of our input comes from a vast network of amateur blogs devoted to topics ranging from Photoshop tips to opinions about UX design.

The problem with this approach is that often the designers who develop the solutions we emulate know a lot more about why and when their solution is appropriate. We latch on to these good ideas without completely understanding them. Ask yourself these questions:

- HTML5 Boilerplate is a very popular HTML/CSS skeleton to start with when developing a site. Do you know what each of the reset (or **normalize.css**) properties do?

- When is a horizontal nav appropriate?

- When is it appropriate to use a text link as opposed to a button?

- When should you not use Modernizr? Do you include it in every project, regardless of what's needed?

- Why are design patterns important?

Rather than trying to stump you, these questions are intended to make you think about why certain technologies or design patterns are considered best practices. If our industry can focus more on *why* and less on *how*, I think we can overcome our penchant for fads and trendsetting.

The point is that we tend to be sucked in by new trends; for example, letterpress type as seen in Figure 2.1. We want to try them out for size, to put another wrench in the toolbox.

Figure 2.1. Letterpress type can be gorgeous, if used with a little subtlety

Generally speaking, slapping "the new shiny thing" on your personal blog is just dandy. Go nuts. Experimentation is what personal sites are for. It only becomes a problem when we end up leaning on these trends; when every new design trick becomes *the* way to do things even if it's inappropriate for the design.

Instead of following trends, we should focus on understanding the fundamental properties of design. Our main purpose as designers is to deliver results to clients that solve their problems and fulfill their needs. We can admire new styles and treatments without trying to wedge them into designs where they're unsuitable. Put simply, if "the new shiny thing" fails to help a client accomplish their goals, it doesn't belong in the design.

The Parable of Cynthia

Let me tell you a little story.

It's about a lovely young girl named Cynthia. Cynthia is 15 and loves the Internet. She adores it. She chats with friends all the time over Skype. Her life *is* Facebook, as is evident in Figure 2.2. For reals. She is tech-savvy and has the Dropbox account to prove it.

Figure 2.2. Bright-eyed Cynthia loves the Web …

Eventually, Cynthia realizes that she's really interested in how all this cool stuff works, so she starts learning HTML and CSS from her high-school teacher. After she graduates from high school, she achieves an undergraduate degree in web design and front-end development. To Cynthia, HTML5 is child's play. CSS3? You've never seen rounded corners like these. jQuery, PHP? You name it; Cynthia is on her way to mastery.

After five years in the field, Cynthia is now an accomplished designer. Hurray for Cynthia! She decides to go back to school and study for her graduate degree in Interaction Design and eventually, her PhD in User Experience. All before she's 35.

Once she completes her formal education, Cynthia takes her 13 years of experience and three degrees, opens her own design firm, rocks the industry for the next 33 years! Along the way, she writes a couple of books and stays on the bleeding edge of design and development. She is a rock star.

After her much-deserved retirement, Cynthia travels the world, speaking about User Experience and best practices—generally making the Web world a better place. She continues to engage with the industry until that final hour when she goes on to the great motherboard in the sky. She lives a long life immersed in code and loving every minute of it.

Cynthia's tale of triumph poses a number of questions. How many of us know an individual like Cynthia? Even barring the greatness of her success, do you know a person who's been in the game for as long as Cynthia? Someone who's been in the web design industry for four or five decades after going three rounds of formal education with degrees in the field, all the way to a PhD?

I'd venture a guess that you answered a resounding "no." Our industry hasn't been around long enough to create people like Cynthia! HTML has only been publicly available since 1991. CSS's initial release was in 1996. Even if Cynthia was involved with the Web from its earliest origins as a CERN project in 1980 (which would be difficult for a high-school student), she'd only be about fifty years old. She'd have nearly another two decades to run her business and only be ready to retire around 2030.

I use this tale to illustrate the youth of the web industry. We are still taking our first steps into comprehending the complexities of web-based interaction. It's okay that we're feeling around in the dark some of the time. It also explains why we all learn from each other. The point is that any kind of formal education focusing on the theory of interaction, design, and user experience is hard to find. We spend a lot of time coming up with our own theories and testing them in the wild.

In short, we have very little history. The breakneck pace that we've been on for the last couple of decades makes it feel like our occupation has been around forever. Well, it hasn't.

 Finding Research

If you are looking for research about design and user experience, I'd recommend hitting up the websites of your local library or college campus. Often, you can access their databases and find articles from peer-reviewed journals that you won't find anywhere else. In my experience, schools have a better selection of databases, but you might need a student or faculty login to access their materials. Approach the design or art departments and request information.

Public libraries are a great resource for information, too. They also have access to databases of peer-reviewed journals, but the selection probably won't be as good.

A few great journals to look for are *The International Journal of Design*, *Human Factors*, *Human-Computer Interaction*, and the *Journal of Computer Science*. They cover a lot of ground, so these four journals could easily get you started. Enjoy!

Lucky for us, other industries have put immense amounts of time and research into the various components of what we do. Artists and print designers have been crafting stunning visuals for centuries. Scientists have studied everything to death (my, how they like to write papers!). Reams of pages have been written about heuristics, ergonomics, aesthetics, user experience, interface artifacts, and any other topic you can think of.

We have lots of knowledge to draw from. So, let's take a trip down memory lane and explore our origins.

Art History 101: Just Enough to Be Dangerous

Most visual trends in web design have a foundation in styles and movements of the past, which all carry their own ideas and character as Figure 2.3 shows. Art movements and styles tend to be a response to what came before. They try to answer questions that the old styles failed to do. This means that each style is intended to support certain ideas.

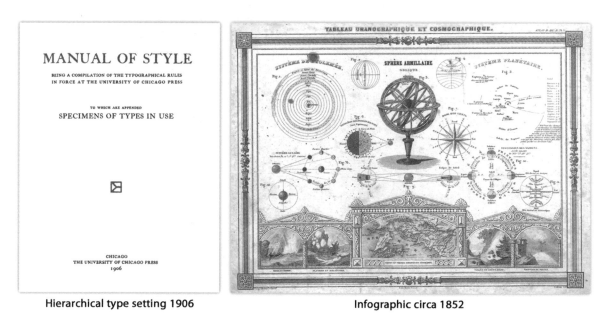

Hierarchical type setting 1906   **Infographic circa 1852**

Figure 2.3. Learning about the past can help you deal with the present

I could go down through the ages and tell you about every important artistic achievement—from cave paintings to the crisp lines of the latest BMW—but you'd probably chuck this book across the room. Instead, I'll throw a detailed timeline on the Web (where else?)[1] and note the highlights most relevant to web design.

Now I'll focus on three movements in art and design, then finish up with a discussion about the importance of print for web designers.

---

[1] http://http://www.sitepoint.com/books/process1/timeline/

Arts and Crafts

The **Arts and Crafts movement** was mostly a response to industrialized fabrication and the machined qualities of manufactured items. An example is shown in Figure 2.4.[2] It flourished during the late 19th century and into the early years of the 20th. The idea behind it was to return to an appreciation of natural materials and handicraft.

Figure 2.4. The Arts and Crafts movement sought to rediscover the natural beauty of handicraft

The Arts and Crafts philosophy influenced more than just image design. At its heart, the movement was a repudiation of the effects of industrialization on art. Furniture, textiles, architecture, books, and wallpapers were all items that Arts and Crafts designers targeted, but it was also an approach

---

[2] William Morris, *Tulip and Willow* (1873)

to life. Communities were built around the philosophy, and many great thinkers dedicated themselves to its preservation.

William Morris, Charles Rennie Mackintosh, and John Ruskin (along with many others) were leading figures of the movement and established many of its design motifs. Morris is probably best known for his wallpaper patterns and tapestry designs, which are incredible studies in muted color harmonies. Mackintosh was an architect and painter. John Ruskin's writing influenced the movement's ideas.

Florid patterns and superfluous detail abound in Arts and Crafts designs because many designers of the style were also interested in medieval art and natural forms. This emphasis on detail and organic shapes later became a primary influence for the better-known Art Deco and Art Nouveau movements.

The Arts and Crafts movement is relevant because contemporary web design shares some of the same goals. We're trying to overcome the limitations of our medium to create designs that have some connection to reality and to our users. We go about creating that connection differently, but the essence of seeking tactile elements that have an emotional impact is the same. The significance of individuality, nature, and handicraft is very real in the web design industry.

The Arts and Crafts movement was a response to the machine-fabricated products of early industrialization. Arts and Crafts designers wanted to reinforce the importance of materials and nature. Until recently, web design shared a similar problem. Designs were restricted by the technology, being flat and digital. Now many of us are trying to create richly textured designs that "feel" like real materials. We are cultivating an appreciation for simulating reality. Do you see the similarity? Arts and Crafts designers were responding to an aesthetic imposed by developing technology. Web designers face a comparable problem and solution.

Minimalism

Minimalism is an attempt to reduce a work to its bare essentials, to remove all ornamentation so that only the structure is left, such as in the work of Richard Serra in Figure 2.5.

Figure 2.5. Minimalism can be hard to understand in its purest form

Reduce a painting and you have canvas and paint. Reduce a web design and what do you get? Figure 2.6, that's what!

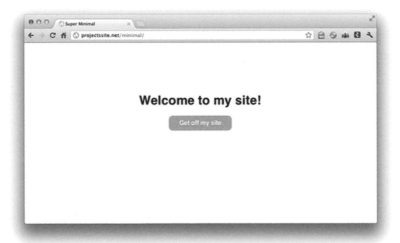

Figure 2.6. The most minimal site ever

Arguably, any site can be reduced to nothing more than text and links. Perhaps I should say content and links. Maybe add a few lines to reinforce the grid structure of the page. And a couple of colors just to brand it a little. Sound familiar? You probably know quite a few designers who work this way. Heck, you may be one. Tons of us take this approach: add what has to be included, and then sprinkle on a bit of flavor.

We want it clean, clean, clean!

It's hard to put a date on Minimalism because the aesthetic is fairly universal. Piet Mondrian was painting lines and primary colors in the 1920s and '30s. A minimal aesthetic has been around for far longer than that, but it gained serious traction in fine art in the 1960s with Geometric Abstraction, which, as its name suggests, utilized regular shapes in abstract ways. Figure 2.7 shows an example of this form.[3]

Figure 2.7. Geometric Abstraction

Artists like Barnett Newman and Tony Smith, though also connected with other art movements, were creating highly reductionist paintings and sculptures characterized by expansive fields of flat color, and simple lines and shapes (sound familiar?). I've seen Newman's *Stations of the Cross* and was truly awed by the grandeur of those paintings. Minimalism can be difficult to understand, but the best minimal works certainly leave an impression.

Minimalism spans multiple art forms and is still widely appreciated for its reductionist sensibilities, though it is often viewed as a quality of design instead of a philosophy for design.

In web design, the term "clean" is largely synonymous with minimal. A design with clean lines is usually highly structured, makes smart use of white space, and is likely devoid of strong imagery.

---

[3] Theo van Doesburg, *Simultaneous Counter-Composition* (1929-30)

Many of the designers I've spoken to (not all, mind you) aim to create sites that don't interfere with the content. A content-centric approach to web design is excellent, but I find it disappointing when "not interfering with content" equates to a white screen with text and little else.

I take issue with this, because minimal web design can be so much more. We can take a page from the book of fine art and develop a much richer understanding of the minimal aesthetic instead of focusing on just one interpretation of it. Lots of minimal art is full of rich color and complex structure. There's no reason why our minimal designs can't consist of the same.

Minimal design can be a great vehicle for focusing attention. By eliminating superfluous design elements, we're forced to consider structure and content almost exclusively. Economy, layout, emphasis, and color become that much more important. Fewer items on the page means that their relationship to each other becomes vital.

Modernism

I really want to talk about Postmodernism, but in order to do that you need to talk about Modernism first. **Modernism** (with a capital M) is difficult to define because the qualities and chronologies vary depending on the medium. Modernism in literature differs to Modernism in art or design. Still, a few characteristics are generally common between all branches of Modernism, and they're relevant to what we do as contemporary designers because they define our current understanding of design.

In my opinion, Modernism can be identified by three factors:

- Modernism rejected the historical emphasis on realism and tradition espoused by earlier forms or art, such as those seen in Figure 2.8.

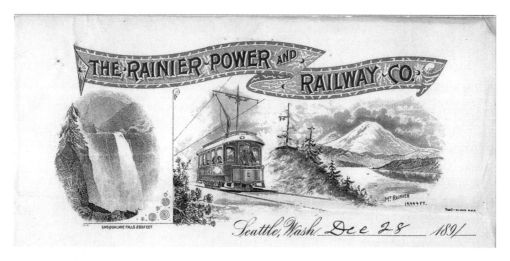

Figure 2.8. Design before Modernism

- Modernism introduced the idea that structure and fundamental elements were the real building blocks of creativity. In art and design, this meant that works could be appreciated from a formal and structural standpoint. Before Modernism, the quality of an artwork was measured by the artist's skill at accurately representing reality. In other words, do the figures in a painting look real? Are the landscapes detailed and accurate? Today, instead of just focusing on the technical skill of the artist, we evaluate art and design by assessing the relationships between color, shape, form, structure, and so on. Our current understanding of the elements and principles of design originated with Modernism.

Modernism encouraged personal expression and artistic integrity. A lot of Modernist work is inaccessible to the average viewer because there's often very little reference to what the user can identify. Minimalist art might just be a slab of concrete or a canvas coated in a solid field of color. Abstract art might be based on a real object, but have no resemblance to it at all. To the untrained eye, works like this can seem strange, as Figure 2.9 shows.

Figure 2.9. Design after Modernism

In the early 20th century, schools like Bauhaus and De Stijl were the first to teach the Modernist aesthetic in a formal setting. Teaching any subject requires a common language and set of theories; otherwise, nothing can be communicated from teacher to student. Much of the design principles that we employ today were formed in early schools like these. If you went to a school for design in the last hundred years, it's Modernism you have to thank for your education. All that talk about form versus function and design sensibilities comes from this era.

In fine art, Impressionism, Cubism, Fauvism, Minimalism, and Abstract Expressionism—the big "isms"—are all Modernist movements, and that's just naming a few. Modernists were trying to understand the fundamentals of art creation and to depart from the traditional appreciation for realism. Minimalism was about reducing art to its most basic structure. Cubism was about temporality and psychology. Abstract Expressionism was about the medium and the process. What they all have in common is their quest for a new way of making art that was independent of traditions while creating a deeper understanding of its fundamental properties.

We've all had teachers and art directors tell us that as designers, we are really communicators. Our aim is to make the message clear. Our designs are supposed to be structured and dynamic. We are taught to emphasize typography, shape, and form. We will worship, yes, worship, Paul Rand![4] All of that is very Modernist.

Postmodernism

Now for the fun bit. **Postmodernism** is a direct response to Modernism. It's way too big a topic for this book, but I'm going to give it a whirl anyway. It has its roots in philosophers like Kant and Descartes, and relates to everything from politics to the nature of reality. It's, like, deep and stuff.

I'll skip that side of it, but I will say that from an artistic standpoint, Postmodernism is the art of the subjective. It's about putting yourself into the work. From a formal standpoint, Postmodernism shares the same ideas as Modernism: it emphasizes formality over tradition, personal expression over accessibility, and conceptual ideas over representational imagery.

The real difference is that Modernism was an exploration of the fundamental properties of art and design. Postmodernism is the combination of all those properties in the service of expressing an artist's personal vision. I'm sure some art historians will argue the finer points of both movements, but for our purposes, I think we've distinguished them enough. Think about it this way: Modernism was about formal qualities in art and design. For instance, Cubism was an incredibly important movement in art because it showed that the representational aspects of imagery could be used to convey so much more than reality. But most of its value was actually in thinking up the idea of Cubism.

As an artistic movement, Cubism was revelatory for artists because it gave them a glimpse of the possibilities of what could be communicated through art. But once the idea was conveyed and understood, it's questionable whether making Cubist art became relevant anymore. Does anyone need to continue making Cubist paintings?

To explore that question, let me tell you another story. You love art and design, but let's say you want to try something new. You throw away your computer (I know, I wince inside as I write these

---

[4] For those out of the loop, Mr. Rand was a graphic designer famous for corporate logo designs such as IBM, UPS, and Westinghouse.

words) and your wireframes and you buy oil paints. All your friends think you've gone bonkers, but you're determined to be a painter. That's you in Figure 2.10.

Figure 2.10. A budding artist

At first you try painting landscapes. You buy some Bob Ross DVDs and learn how to paint "happy trees," and for a while, you're content to learn all that Bob has to offer.[5] You amass an impressive portfolio of oval-shaped paintings of cottages and streams, but after a while you begin to find it all a bit boring and formulaic. You decide to try a new approach.

Next, you try your hand at figure painting, so you hire a couple of nude models but it soon loses its shine. In no time at all, you realize that figure painting is hard and models are expensive, so you ax that venture too. Now you are at a loss. You've dedicated your life to painting. You are committed—nay, devoted—to the craft! Well, what now? You've tried landscapes and figure painting. Both flopped, so what's an artist to do?

Your immensely successful friend, Cynthia, sees that you are down. She wants to help, so she takes you to a Picasso exhibition where you see your first Cubist painting. Instantly, you are hooked. You love everything about it: the marks, the muted color, the strangely proportioned figures. "My figure paintings sort of look like that already," you think. "I'm now a Cubist!"

You've found your muse and spend the next few months putting together a dozen paintings. You're thrilled and elated by your work, so you line them up in your studio and invite Cynthia over to take a gander. You hand her a glass of Champagne and ask her what she thinks. Cynthia looks at the paintings for a moment. "You know," she says, "these paintings are very well executed." You glow with pride. "The marks are nicely textured, the colors are rich, and the people are distorted to perfection." You are positively vibrating with good feelings. "These paintings *look* like Cubist

---

[5] Bob Ross was an American painter best known for his TV show *The Joy of Painting*.

paintings, even though they aren't. Cubism has been dead for, like, 80 years. These are just pretty pictures."

Ouch. She was fairly tough on you. The imaginary version of me will definitely buy the imaginary version of you a beer.

This example may sound harsh, but you can be creative without forming a brand new artistic movement every time you are. It's okay to make paintings in the Cubist style, or designs that have Cubist references. We can borrow from older styles without impunity. Still, you have to admit she has a point. Why rehash old ideas? If Modernism was about discovering the fundamentals of art and design, what do you do after the discoveries have been made?

What you (the imaginary version of you, that is) failed to realize is that all art and design has context. Picasso developed Cubism at a time when the understanding of art and design was completely different. His work reshaped the very idea of art. If you try to make Cubist paintings today, you're just being derivative. Modernism has given us a common language for design. There's no need to reproduce the art and design that Modernists created to discover that common language. Instead, we just use it. The principles and elements of design are common knowledge and act as a baseline for quality in the creative field. We are at a point where the objective fundamentals are well established. Good design and art goes beyond simply exploring the medium.

Postmodernism is an attempt to utilize the formal properties exposed by Modernism to create emotion and personal experience. If you (again, the imaginary you) want to be a painter, you need to spin the idea of Cubism and paint your interpretation of it, or apply the aesthetic of Cubism in some new way.

The point is that Postmodernism is inescapable. You may be unaware of it, but if you're doing anything creative with your work, you are almost certainly a postmodern designer. We don't design in a vacuum. Everything that we do, creative or otherwise, exists in the context of all the work that's come before. When we copy older styles and motifs, we are always affected by the context that they create. Every time you make a whimsical reference to older styles in your work, you create a context. So, if you're going down that road, you might as well understand all the references you're making. The fact that we reference past styles and tailor them to our own purposes is a postmodern approach to design. It pays to know your place in design history. Where does your work fit into Figure 2.11?

Figure 2.11. Every movement is connected—they blend in some places and break free in others

Newspapers: How do you surf the Web on those?

We all know the printed form is dying. Newspapers are shrinking as their advertising revenue dries up and content migrates to the Web; meanwhile, tablet computers and smartphones chant a low, self-satisfied death knell for them. At least, that's what all the web designers I know are saying. It might be true. Print may really be dying. Ebooks and handheld devices may eventually replace books and newspapers.

But even if this is print's final hour, the world can take heart in knowing that it will live on through our work. The truth is that we owe the print medium a great deal of gratitude, whether it goes the way of the dinosaur or not. Almost all the design patterns and theories we employ were originally developed for print. The inescapable truth is that for a very long time we've all been print designers masquerading as interactive designers. We have benefited greatly from the print industry's explorations of information architecture, visual hierarchy, and communication. The Internet is just a massive collection of linked text documents, and all our knowledge about displaying text comes from print.

Column Grids

Column grids are the backbone of every magazine and newspaper. Newspapers may look like nothing more than immense walls of ink, but a lot of time and thought went into deciding the width of those columns. Someone labored over the proportion between the vertical and horizontal gutters. Centuries of trial and error have perfected the science of laying out huge amounts of text on a page and still keeping it legible.

As seen in Figure 2.12, contemporary web design is almost always based on column-grid theory, though the subtleties of baseline rhythm are often difficult to manage with dynamic content. We owe the most basic structural consideration in web design to newspapers.

Figure 2.12. Column grids give structure and form to website content

Typography

Obviously, **typography** is a major component of print design that we've modified for better screen legibility. Because serifs fare poorly on pixelated screens, entire suites of fonts have been created to provide a better experience for readers.

Even so, it's impossible to escape our print past. The terminology we use to discuss typesetting has its history in print. The term "leading," which refers to the vertical space between lines of text, is derived from the real pieces of lead that typesetters placed between rows of movable type to keep them in place.

Information Hierarchy

Print has taught us how to create an **information hierarchy** for our content. The multilevel h tags in HTML (h1, h2, and so on)—seen in Figure 2.13—have a direct correlation to the multilevel section headers in almost every book, magazine, and newspaper the world over. We'll dive much deeper into structure in the section called "Structure and Form" in Chapter 4.

Figure 2.13. h tags and semantic markup help create hierarchical information

I mention print here because I'd encourage more web designers to study print design in detail. Many of the problems we face have concrete solutions in the form of print design. While it was never intended for the kind of interaction that exists online, we've adapted much of print to suit our needs. In this case, there's no need to reinvent the wheel. Print has the answers to some of our most pressing questions about visual communication. I think we'd be fools not to learn from centuries of exploration and technical advancement.

The New Kids

So far, we've only talked about the visual side of design communication, but the fact is that we aren't designing newspapers or making Cubist paintings (no matter how badly we might want to). Web design comes with a set of complications that didn't exist before the advent of computers and screen-based devices. The Web is becoming increasingly dynamic, so our designs have to accommodate ever-changing content. We have to design templates that can be used to build pages that we have no way of knowing will exist. Our designs are interactive, which means that we have to design multiple states for parts of our designs.

Designing multiple states for a design element can be as simple as designing the inactive, active, and hover states for a button. Then again, it can mean designing dynamically generated content blocks, popovers, modal windows, and galleries, just to name a few. We must consider the dynamics of our designs, in order to create satisfying interactive experiences.

In addition to the dynamics of web design, users are viewing our work on devices of varying sizes and pixel dimensions. We therefore have to accommodate multiple browsers, operating systems, and form factors. As print has no solutions for these problems, we've had to branch off into other disciplines to find what we need. We'll talk about these other disciplines later, but I want to introduce them here because they're essential to creating compelling designs and experiences. Being creative requires an understanding of what's possible in our medium and what's necessary to communicate effectively with users.

These new disciplines are helping our industry to at least ask the right questions and search for ways of finding answers.

Interaction Design

I find interaction design to be endlessly interesting because it is all about behavior. People who use websites have behavior. Interactive media also has behavior. **Interaction design** attempts to pair those two sets of behaviors to produce compelling experiences.

Interaction design is concerned with creating usability by understanding the user's behavior and controlling the site's behavior. Historically, this practice has its roots in the 1980s and human-computer interaction (HCI). The invention of the personal computer created an interest in how humans interact with digital devices. People approached the exploration of HCI from many angles. Those interested in the human aspect of HCI rallied behind a special branch of the cognitive science called Cognitive and Software Ergonomics. **Cognitive ergonomics** is focused on understanding and directing human mental processes such as perception, memory, and reasoning. **Software ergonomics** is about accommodating the natural cognitive and physical capabilities of users. Other research focused on hardware and physical interaction. HCI is fascinating because of its complexity, but it's a little beyond the scope of this book. For our purposes, I'll mainly be focusing on the design of web interface interactions when I mention interaction design.

User Experience Design

User experience design refers to all aspects of a person's experience when interacting with a product or service. It doesn't refer only to websites, though that's the context where we'll most often discuss it in this book. User experience design can refer to any experience.

In his book, *The Design of Everyday Things*, (New York: Basic, 2002) Donald A. Norman spends a long time talking about the usability of doors and light switches. Norman coined the term "user experience" in the 1990s, and intended it to include a person's physical, emotional, and cognitive experience. You can think of it as an umbrella term that covers interface design, interaction design, information architecture, and surface design. It's the whole enchilada.

An emphasis on user experience (UX) often leads us to ask questions that might not arise if we were only designing for content. We are forced to empathize with the people who'll eventually be face to face with our designs and assumptions. Quite a lot of research has gone into this subject, and we'll talk about it more throughout the book.

Condensed Fonts, Horn-rimmed Glasses, and Flow Charts

This chapter was intended to illustrate that we are part of a larger timeline of design, and that it pays to know where we fit in that timeline. We have a lot of growing to do, and I'm sure as we learn to better understand the medium, our roles will change.

Better design calls for a deeper understanding of all the disciplines that surround our work. We have to go beyond the visual stuff, even if it's the most fun! We spend so much time with our noses to the grindstone that we sometimes forget to go outside our comfort zone and explore what everyone else is doing. Let me tell you, artists and designers have been hard at work for centuries. Learning from their insights and brilliance should be second nature to us.

I trust that this little exploration into the past has helped to illustrate the value of the history we share with our predecessors. Every graphical style that we employ in our designs has its roots in art and design from the past. The more we know about that past, the better it can serve our needs.

Here's what I hope you've taken away from this chapter:

- Knowledge is power and we have lots of it. It would be a shame to let it go to waste.

- Our industry is in its infancy, but growing at an unprecedented speed. Now is the time to take as much as we can from the work of our predecessors.

- Web design is more than just visual design. Interaction, interface, and experience design are becoming increasingly relevant as we grow more aware of their importance, so brush up—you want to be creating more than just a pretty picture.

- Cynthia is kind of awesome, but mean. Avoid letting her critique your paintings.

- We have to know where we've been to understand where we are going.

Gathering Resources: That Rucksack Has a Lot of Pockets

So far we've covered a lot of ground, though we're yet to cover the gritty details of applying what we've learned from the first two chapters. In this chapter, we'll address how we can start to build the visual language of our design by gathering all the bits and pieces to use as reference materials.

We'll begin gathering design resources for our Spectrumagic project for two reasons:

- To organize the intended visuals for our design and compile a set of source materials
- To communicate our plans to the client

All the materials we'll gather in this chapter will be in an attempt to satisfy these two requirements. We want to align our expectations with those of the client. The fact is, many problems can arise during the design process to disrupt the project. Changes in the project's requirements can make it necessary to rework designs. User feedback can cause a project to pivot in another direction. Budget adjustments can cause the scale of a project to grow or shrink. Some problems are hard to anticipate, but we can do our best to mitigate the problems that arise from poor communication. If a mockup is rejected because you used the wrong colors, you probably started the design before you had all the details.

By answering these questions and building a library of visual resources to communicate with the client, we can start a collaboration that will avoid frustration and lead us to a great design.

Communicating with Clients

"If it's a case of the client [having] a set budget, and you could attribute some of it to wireframing and some of the budget to content and content review … I'd rather use the money that we would've used for wireframes, which I'm going to do anyway, because I do it on paper, to sort out your content, because it's a mess."

—Sarah Parmenter

Most of us love to dive into a project. Sure, the blank white canvas of a new Photoshop document can be daunting, but the beginning of any new project is exciting. Pushing pixels around is fun, and we know that if we go at it long enough, we'll come up with some amazing angle. However, it's right here, at this most captivating point in the project, that we must show some restraint. Quite a bit should happen before we even think about a new design.

So, let's talk to the client!

Ask Questions

To create designs that satisfy our client's goals, we first need to know the goals. We also have to find out the client's design imperatives, their ideas about what they wants to see, and any restrictions imposed upon the project. Additionally, for each of these, we need to know their opposite. What does the client want to avoid? Where do we have a free hand to work the design the way that we want to? And so on.

Soon, we'll take another look at the Spectrumagic notes that our client sent to us; for now, let's put together a simple **punch list** of necessary details before we begin. This is a rough list that can serve you well in any project. We'll call it our "Need to Know List."

1. Who is the intended audience?
   - What is their age group and demographic?
   - Is the audience computer literate?

2. What brand guidelines must be followed?
   - Are there color or design guidelines?
   - How closely do we need to stick with the brand's identity?
   - What tone do we need to establish?

3. What is the site's intended purpose?
   - Are there marketing goals?
   - Is the client trying to sell a product or service?
   - What are some of the goals that the client hopes to achieve with the site?

4. What is the site's content?

- What is the subject matter of the content?
- Is the content structure complex?
- How much content will be on the site?
- Will the content constantly change or will it be relatively static?

5. What additional restrictions are placed on the project?
   - Does it need to be viewed on legacy browsers or special devices?
   - Will the site be updated internally?
   - Does the site form part of a larger campaign?
   - Does the site need to work in conjunction with other media like print or film?

6. What should we avoid?
   - What is off limits?
   - Should we avoid certain design choices?

7. What is the project budget?
   - Is the amount the client wants to spend realistic for the project's requirements?

8. What is the project timeline and production schedule?
   - Does the client have realistic expectations for how long the project will take to complete?
   - What benchmarks need to be met?
   - What responsibilities will the client be taking?

This list is by no means complete. It serves as a basic starting point for communication between you and the client. You'll probably never be able to anticipate all the questions that need answering over the course of a project, but this is a good place to begin.

Questionnaires

> "I have several philosophies I follow. The first is: 'Never solve the problem you are asked to solve.' It's almost always the wrong problem. What people think is the problem is the symptom. You have to get at what the real root cause is. The Japanese have a philosophy they call: 'The Five Whys.' When I'm called in to solve a problem, I ask, 'Why is that a problem?' Somebody will tell me and I'll again ask, 'Why is that a problem?' They'll tell me and I'll ask, 'Why is that a problem?' Eventually, we reach the real fundamental issue and quite often, if you solve the fundamental issue, the original problem they were having just disappears. It's no longer relevant."
>
> —Donald Norman

You might even find it easier to put a questionnaire together for your clients to fill out. Just use the preceding questions (or whatever you think are relevant) and leave enough room for answers.

Keep in mind that doing it this way has its pros and cons. One benefit is that the client's answers are documented. You could do this yourself during a meeting when asking the client about the project, but having the client fill it out in advance can save you this task. Sometimes, a questionnaire can produce faster answers; however, you'll have to interpret those answers on your own, without the client in front of you.

I find that being able to ask follow-up questions is key to receiving good information. Follow-up questions are difficult to anticipate, because they're a reaction to the client's answer to another question. Since each client is different, follow-up questions are likely to differ from project to project.

Either way, gather as much information as you can as soon as possible. It will save you a headache later in the project. Nothing is more frustrating that creating an amazing design that's completely wrong for the client. By having it's involvement early on in the process, you can try to mitigate problems that arise from poor communication.

What's next?

So far, we've put together our basic list of questions to ask our client. In the case of Spectrumagic, the client has already provided us with a document that lists some of their expectations for the project, which is nice. Not all clients have that much forethought.

Let's take another look at the document to see what questions from our "Need To Know List" have been answered. After that, we'll look at some interesting ways to gather the visual resources we'll use to inform our design and communicate our ideas to the client.

Getting What You Need: Grab Your Compass and Bowie Knife ...

Before we start gathering resources, we should take a second look at the Spectrumagic document that we received from our client. We need to know what problems we're solving, and then put together a simple list of tasks to complete over the course of this chapter. So, here are the bullet points that the client gave us to consider:

- Spectrumagic is an educational site about color. It is a highly interactive and dynamic experience that teaches the reader about the science of visible color and the practical application of color theory.

- It is primarily designed for high-school students, but should be accessible to middle-school students and adults as well.

- It will work on tablet devices and all modern browsers. It will have a tactile feel that promotes interaction.

- It will include extensive content that is broken into two distinct categories: the science of color, and color theory. Each category will have a quiz that users can take to test their knowledge. Half the quiz will comprise multiple-choice questions, and the other half will be an interactive game.

- It will be highly visual and provide some kind of visual feedback about the user's progress through the content.

- It will incorporate the Spectrumagic brand.

> "I think that there are people who are primarily visual designers and their major role is style and polish. You can hand something to them that is mostly [complete], and say, 'We need good iconography. Tie our brand to this page.' I think there is a role for people like that, but I'm much more interested in broader product design, where the designer helps establish the most fundamental product directions. Is this actually the right product for our business? Is our business doing the right thing? Are we selling the right widgets? Asking these questions is part of a designers role."
>
> —Daniel Burka

So much goes into design that it's hard to have a real sense of what we're trying to achieve without realistic goals. Luckily for us, our client has provided us with some solid information.

We know that the site is intended for high-school and middle-school students, so we know our audience. We know the content has two facets: color theory and the science of visual color. We're yet to have all the details about content, but we have a clear starting point.

We know that the site has to be device- and resolution-agnostic; in other words, it needs to work on all devices, independent of resolution or form factor. That's good to know, because we can begin preparing ideas for how the site will handle touch interactions, mouse interactions and smaller resolutions. We might even entertain the idea of serving a different version of the site to smaller devices if doing so will create a better user experience.

We're aware that the client is concerned about interaction. There are two bullet points about interaction: one telling us that the test will have game elements, and another referencing "visual feedback." Because the client has focused on details such as visual feedback, they're likely to have ideas about what this feedback entails; hence, we should ask more questions about it.

Finally, we know some restrictions will be placed on the design by the Spectrumagic brand guidelines. We're yet to see the guidelines, but we know they're coming.

I think we've made a good start having all the information we need to start our design, but it's just a start. Some questions are yet to be answered. I can infer that the site's intended purpose is to educate teenagers about color, but what tone should the site have? What are some of the client's goals? Why does the site exist at all? What should we avoid when designing the Spectrumagic site?

How strict are the Spectrumagic brand guidelines? What kind of games are they imagining for the quizzes? Let's begin gathering materials we can use to help frame our questions to the client.

Research: What's the competition doing?

Once we have some information from the client, we can take a few minutes to see what other designers have done with similar projects. For instance, Spectrumagic is a learning site for teens. Plenty of other sites are dedicated to educating teenagers about a wide variety of topics. We can look to them to see any trends in information architecture or organization that might help us with our site.

An educational site like Khan Academy[1] structures its lessons into sequences that comprise very short videos that are easy to digest. Each short video builds on the previous one, so a student with minimal knowledge on a subject can start from the beginning and work through a large amount of information relatively quickly. This structure also works for students who do have some base knowledge, because it allows them to easily skip ahead to the more advanced lessons. Though it's unlikely that we'll be using video for our site, we can break all the content into small, easily understood pieces, so that no one page is overwhelming.

Treehouse[2] is another site that's relevant to our project. It's an educational site for web professionals that teaches designers and developers a range of topics about their craft. Where it connects with the Spectrumagic project is in the use of game-like elements. Treehouse engages its students by treating each set of videos as a task. If students complete all the lessons and finishes a short quiz, they are awarded a "badge," which is an icon that shows their progress. This is a fun way to keep track of students' results while also challenging them.

Perhaps we can apply a similar idea in our project. We could search for sites that have features or structures that can help us with Spectrumagic, and I encourage you to do so at every opportunity. Again, remember to look at other media as well. Videos, games, and textbooks can be rich sources of inspiration for how a site might work. Explore every possibility.

Check Your Files: Dredging Up the Past

When presented with a new project, my first inclination is to look through my design portfolio and see if I've addressed similar problems. I want to evaluate the solutions I developed for earlier projects and see if they apply to the new one. I'm not advocating the repurposing of old designs, but there's no sense in reinventing the wheel. Taking a look at past projects can be inspiring and remind us of ideas that we've forgotten, such as some of mine in Figure 3.1.

---

[1] www.khanacademy.org
[2] www.teamtreehouse.com

Figure 3.1. Past work can reveal details that might be useful in a current undertaking

As I see it, Spectrumagic has three fairly novel challenges:

- Spectrumagic has games (or "game-like elements") built into the general content.

- It is supposed to provide consistent feedback to users as they progress through the material.

- It has two unique but related subjects that need to be given equal prominence: the science of color and color theory.

I can usually find a design with similar requirements to act as a jumping-off point for a new project. For instance, I've created games with both Flash and jQuery UI in the past. Maybe I can take a look at those projects for some ideas about how to handle the Spectrumagic design. Since the client is yet to specify the kind of games they want to see, I think we can make a few creative suggestions.

For ADCO Design's 2010 Thanksgiving ecard, I created a simple platform game called Flight to entertain their clients. Flight is a side-scrolling platform game, shown in Figure 3.2, where the player is a fattened turkey trying to gather enough balloons to escape from all the hungry Thanksgiving diners.

Figure 3.2. Previous projects can be used to demonstrate ideas and features to clients

We probably won't create a platform game for Spectrumagic, but if Spectrumagic needs keyboard controls, I could use Flight to demonstrate the flow of views to the client. Flight does use a simple pattern of views to handle introducing users to the game controls. This may sound like a small detail to communicate, but we are gathering all the materials that we might need to explain ourselves.

I've also located a couple of posters I did way back in college. They are colorful, minimal designs based on the rainbow, as you can see in Figure 3.3. They aren't very good, as posters go, but they do have a strong visual style that shows off the colors really well.

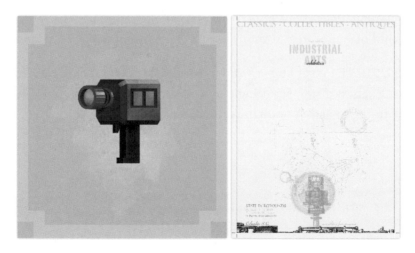

Figure 3.3. Never discount anything as a source for design; I made these posters when I was still in school

I like the minimal aesthetic, because I think it will create a great backdrop for content, and I'm assuming the content will be colorful and complex. Like many designers, I quickly start mulling over ideas for how I think the site should look. Sometimes, we find the assets that support those ideas; sometimes we don't. In this case, I want to show the posters to the client in order to see how they feel about the minimal approach I'm considering.

Organization is essential to keeping a project in order. I keep a folder just for reference material because I want to keep it separate from the image assets that I'll use to create the design. Figure 3.4 presents the structure that I'm using to organize the Spectrumagic project.

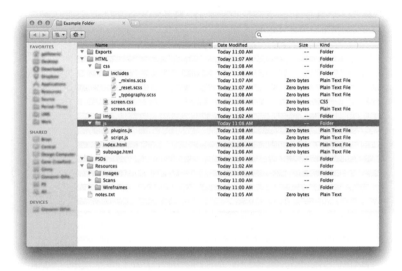

Figure 3.4. My filing system is simple so that I can always find what I'm looking for

Remember, we're gathering references for our clients and ourselves. There's no need to get fancy with how we record those references. In **notes.txt**, I write down the URL where Flight is publicly visible, and take a number of screenshots to record all the states I want to demonstrate to the client.

The posters are simple. I just export them as **.jpg**s. Finally, I take all the images and drop them into my **Reference** folder, adding a couple of comments to **notes.txt** to record what their purpose. This simple way of capturing my thoughts is ideal when I've been working on a project for a number of weeks and am unable to remember what I was thinking when I'd just started.

Color Palettes

There are excellent resources available when seeking color palettes. I often like to experiment with my own variations before going to other resources for color, but I'll briefly discuss my favorite online color resources before we move on to the Spectrumagic color palette.

Kuler

Adobe has a terrific site for manipulating and sharing color palettes called Kuler,[3] seen in Figure 3.5.

---

[3] kuler.adobe.com

Figure 3.5. Kuler is a nifty tool for creating color palettes

Kuler (pronounced "cooler") has everything you could ask for in a color palette tool. Check out Figure 3.6.

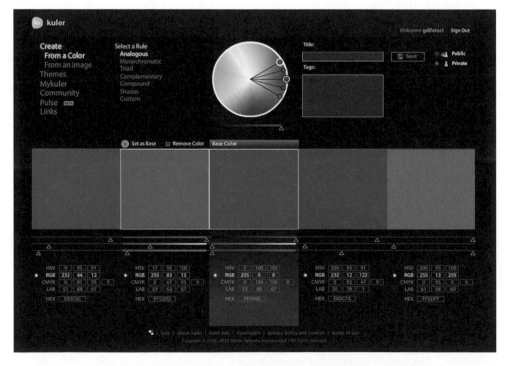

Figure 3.6. Kuler gives you very fine control over every facet of your palette

You can generate a palette from an image. You can choose one color and a color relationship, and Kuler will create a palette by adjusting other colors to fit the relationship. You can tweak your color palette via HSB, RGB, CMYK, or LAB color spaces. Finally, you can save your colors as Adobe Swatch Exchange (ASE) files for use in Photoshop and Illustrator, both of which give you even more tools for tweaking and mixing colors.

Kuler is also a community where you can search for other designers' color palettes to use if you want to skip making your own. I love Kuler, and have used it since I was in school. I'd recommend giving it a whirl if you've never tried it. It's a great tool for any designer's toolkit.

COLOURlovers

COLOURlovers[4] also has a color palette tool, but COLOURlovers is so much more than Kuler: it is a vibrant community of designers and artists, and has user-generated patterns, vectors, colors, palettes, and articles, too. I primarily use COLOURlovers to explore work being generated by other designers, as shown in Figure 3.7.

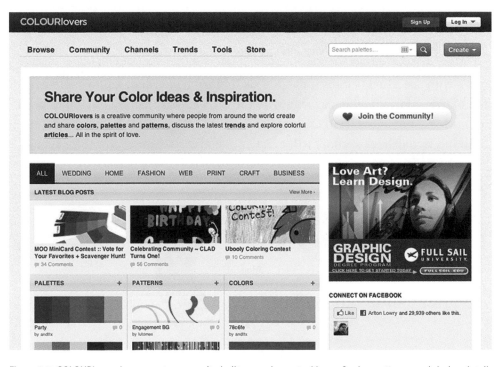

Figure 3.7. COLOURlovers has a great community built around a mutual love of color, patterns, and design details

Not everything at COLOURlovers is of the highest quality, but an amazing amount of the content is stellar. Definitely take some time to peruse the massive library of cool design details.

---

[4] http://www.colourlovers.com/

My only caveat to talking about Kuler and COLOURlovers is that they are no substitute for a good understanding of color. I mostly use them to export my **.ase** (Adobe Swatch Exchange) files, but I make palettes with all my painting history in mind. If you find it difficult to create palettes without these tools, you should probably try to broaden your understanding of color theory.

Brand Colors

Deciding on a color palette requires more than exploring possible combinations for the interface design. Brand requirements will force us to use certain colors in prescribed ways. We should never deviate from the brand guidelines, else we risk damaging the client's identity and creating a design that is out of place with existing and future designs.

Spectrumagic will have a set of primary and secondary brand colors. The logo will be bright and use many colors, but we'll choose three for primary branding: #cf00ff (a rich violet), #ff5a00 (a deep orange), and #00ffb5 (an ice-cream green), as shown in Figure 3.8.

Figure 3.8. Spectrumagic's three primary brand colors

Spectrumagic's color palette is an example of a **secondary triad**. Red, yellow, and blue form the primary triad of the color wheel because they're the only colors that are unable to be created by mixing other colors. They are a triad because they are equidistant on the color wheel, shown in Figure 3.9. Mixing two primary colors will create a secondary color of the color wheel.

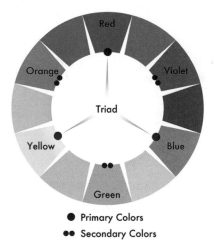

Figure 3.9. The primary colors form a color triad, as do the secondary colors

The fact that the Spectrumagic brand colors form a triad is handy, because we might be able to work that combination into the content or the games. However, we need to consider what impact such bright colors will have on the design. We know that the content will be full of color, and we want our users to not confuse design elements with content, so we may need to minimize the use of the brand colors in our site design.

I suspect that we need to use a fairly achromatic (which essentially means "without color") palette for the interface design. We can treat the Spectrumagic brand colors as accents—bright flashes of saturated color—throughout the design to create interest and focus. This way, we'll avoid muddying our design with a bunch of colors that are competing with one another. We can maintain color harmony by keeping a tight rein on the use of bright color.

To generate my muted palette, I start in Kuler with my branded colors and heavily desaturate them. I then tweak the colors a bit so that I have a range of warm and cool grays based on branded colors. Finally, I add a couple of completely neutral grays of different values to add variety to the palette. I only spend a bit of time doing this because the colors could easily change while the design is taking shape.

Once I've saved the palette to my Kuler profile, I download an Adobe Swatch Exchange file for use in Photoshop. This palette is designed to serve as a counterpoint for the Spectrumagic brand colors and should create a nice, muted foundation for our content.

Now that we've made some basic decisions about colors, we can move on to gathering assets for our mood boards.

Mood Boards

Mood boards are tools for communication. Keep in mind that they're not final products, so avoid spending a lot of time laying them out and prettying them up. Mood boards are more like thumbnails than real designs, only instead of being quick sketches of possible layouts, they're quick collages of possible design elements. No need to worry about the intricacies of design just yet.

A good mood board should do the following.

First, a mood board should display a collection of visual elements and motifs that will be present in the design. Generally, that means a mood board should include examples of the typography, color palette, patterns, shapes, symbols, and imagery that will be used in the design. I start with branded items if I have them, as you can see in Figure 3.10, and then add the rest of the materials later.

Figure 3.10. Start with branded materials to avoid conflicting with the client's identity

Second, a mood board should provide enough visual information to explain our design intentions to the client. It should provide items about which the client can make comments, as in Figure 3.11. Even generic answers like "I like the direction" or "Could we use a different typeface?" are helpful at this point.

Figure 3.11. Mood boards can be used to feel out a client's opinions about your visual ideas

For Spectrumagic, I'm going to create a digital mood board, though you could make a paper collage if you want. I find it easier to scan in printed materials—magazine clippings, newspapers, and so on—and then digitally collage them in Photoshop. By hiding layers and adding new images, I can create several variations of the mood board in very little time. Another feature Photoshop offers is the ability to resize materials; elements can be scaled appropriately and evaluated in a more realistic context.

Mood boards created on a computer lack the tactile and lush qualities of real materials, but at least they reflect how the user will actually experience the visuals: on screen.

Learning from Other Industries

Sorry if I'm belaboring the point, but I do think we have a lot to learn from other creative industries. Interactive design is a synthesis of many art forms. Fine art, photography, writing, illustration, and animation all have roles to play in our designs. Each of these disciplines has practices that have been developed over time to ease the creative process and create amazing products. Figure 3.12 shows two such practices that I think will eventually play a greater role in design.

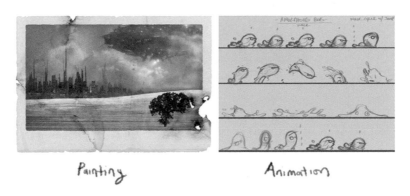

Figure 3.12. Other industries have a lot of insight to offer interactive designers

Storyboards

Storyboards are basically comic strips that are used to tell a narrative; they're probably more well-known in the movie industry, where they outline a story of a film before it's shot. In this sense, they help the film crew to visualize the shots by transforming a script (all text) into a story in pictures. They also play a large role in the creation of animated films and video games.

For interactive design, storyboards can be used to tell the entire arc of the design: how it will flow, how it will be structured, how the user will move from one content area to another, and how a responsive layout will change at each breakpoint. Storyboards can also be used to explain smaller elements, like drop-downs with multiple layers, or other dynamic and interactive elements. Basically, they're useful for showing any kind animation.

A storyboard is a tool for communication in much the same way as our mood board. Mood boards are created to demonstrate visual considerations to the client. Interaction, animation, and state also need to be communicated to the client, and storyboards are a great way of quickly illustrating the complexities of a design before it's created, as Figure 3.13 shows.

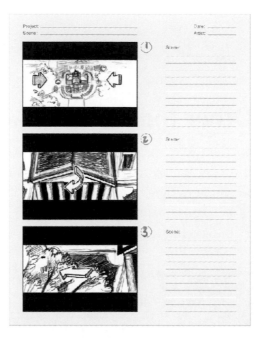

Figure 3.13. This is part of a storyboard showing the "camera path" of a Flash animation

By creating a storyboard, we force ourselves to think about how our designs will play out with interaction. This saves us having to recreate parts of our designs because we forgot to think through how elements in the design might eventually be used. Storyboards can be simple thumbnails in a sequence or more detailed Photoshop sketches. You don't need to be a skilled draftsperson to create useful storyboards either, so long as they clearly illustrate action and interaction, as in Figure 3.14.

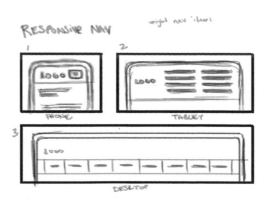

Figure 3.14. Storyboards can also be used to show interaction and transitions like those found in responsive layouts

Take Note

If you do need a storyboard for one of your projects, I recommend laying it out with plenty of room for notes. Whenever you use the storyboard to communicate with the client, you can jot down what they think right next to the frame in question. Trust me—it helps to stave off confusion. I've worked on projects where the client's notes were written as a bulleted list with frame numbers for each note. A detailed list like this is accurate but hard to visualize. Storyboards like the previous one in Figure 3.14 create a direct visual connection between what's shown onscreen and the client's thoughts.

Learning from Your Peers

We've spent some time looking at how animators craft their creative vision. Now it's time to address how we come up with designs! The web design community is impressive when it comes to collaboration and interaction between colleagues. We love to share our work with each other and learn from the accomplishments of our heroes. I think this sense of community stems in part from the fact that we constantly network with each other. We even go so far as to create huge repositories for design, so that all the newbies can learn the ropes a little faster. CSS galleries, design pattern libraries, and technical resources abound in the web design industry. Let's take a look at a few.

I like design galleries because they serve two functions. First, they act as repositories for sites that are, by their very nature, ephemeral and short-lived. Second, they provide budding designers with an opportunity to see web design at its best. Most of the work in these galleries is a combination of technical acumen and solid visual design. We can all learn from our peers' design explorations.

This is just a quick list of some of my favorite galleries and what you can expect from each one:

Unmatched Style (http://unmatchedstyle.com)
The quintessential gallery blog with articles, podcasts, screencasts, and, of course, a gallery of awesome web designs. Its standout feature is that each design is posted with a site review by one of the staff. It is heavily curated.

CSSMania (http://cssmania.com/)
The firehose of design galleries. There isn't much depth to the posts, and there are a lot of them. If you want to see tons of designs and parse through them quickly, this is your site.

Dribbble (http://dribbble.com)
A unique community because its members post snippets instead of the whole design. Lots of the work that's posted is still in progress, which is a nice change from other user-submitted sites. Finally, dribbble.com has an incredibly active community of talented people. If you are looking for serious eye candy, check it out.

Creattica (http://creattica.com)

I like this site because it has everything you could hope for regarding design. Sure, you can find categories for web design, but you can also find T-shirt design, 3D graphics, book cover design, and digital painting. There's even a category for pixel art! I love the variety and wide range of aesthetics.

Typeverything (http://typeverything.com)

An awesome site dedicated to typography, and not just web typography either. Do you want to see calligraphy done with a paint roller? It's there. What about an ampersand made out of a peanut butter and jelly sandwich? Yup.

Abduzeedo (http://abduzeedo.com)

A stellar collection of all things awesome. It's a good mix of design, art, and everything in between. You can also find some interviews, tutorials, and freebies.

This list is just the tip of the iceberg. Thousands of blogs feature great, inspirational material to peruse, not to mention personal portfolios of amazingly talented designers. We've just scratched the surface here. You'll never see everything that your peers have to offer, so try to look at everything you can.

Feeling Resourceful

In this chapter, we have explored the process of gathering source material to help us design Spectrumagic and communicate our ideas to the client. We've also looked at how we can incorporate other industry practices into our process. We created mood boards from branded assets and from the design resources we found while looking through old projects and design galleries. Finally, we put all those assets into our directory setup and made notes about all our ideas.

Now that we have the brain juices flowing on how we want our design to look, we can focus on the structure of the site. In Chapter 4, we'll begin the design process by crafting our preliminary sketches and wireframes. Once we have those in place, we'll be able to go to our client and explain every facet of the project in as much detail as they need.

Chapter **4**

Form and Function

Until now, we've focused mainly on ideas for how to prepare for the design process. We've explored resources for inspiration, techniques that help generate concepts, and methods for organizing our loose visual ideas into deliverables that we can use to communicate with clients.

Once all the planning is done and our initial thoughts have been hashed out, we must start putting together concrete items for design and structure. Eventually, we'll reach the point when we're working in Photoshop (or the browser, if that suits you) and delicately crafting pixel-perfect designs, but first we need to establish what we're designing.

In this chapter we'll discuss thumbnails, wireframes, and grayboxes, which you can see in Figure 4.1. We'll see how they fit into our workflow and what purpose they serve.

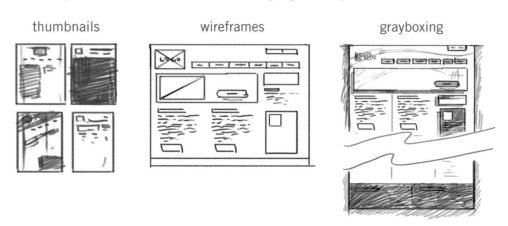

Figure 4.1. Steps in the design process

Why not go straight to Photoshop?

Honestly, it depends on how you prefer to work. No sole process works for everyone, and you may trust your instincts enough to just go for it and hammer out your designs in one sitting. More power to you, if that's the case, but I'd doubt it. Most of us require a little structure to sort out our thoughts and ideas before we can work with them.

I know a number of designers who essentially skip over the predesign phase of the process and go straight to Photoshop for their mockups. They push around pixels until they find a design they're happy with and serve it up to the client. Sometimes it works and the design is accepted, marked up, and shipped out. Sometimes it doesn't.

More often than not, the designers that can make a great design without sketching or wireframing have a fast internal decision-making process. The designer either goes with the first idea, or they have the ability to quickly and decisively accept or reject ideas on the fly. Really, they are going through the same process that I'm outlining, they just do it internally. Either way, a process still takes place when they attack that blank Photoshop canvas.

Be forewarned that usually the ability to solve these problems internally takes a great deal of experience. I just believe that the structure provided by a definite process can help ensure that you give every aspect of the design the attention that it needs and deserves.

Structure and Form

When I refer to the structure of a design, I'm talking about two things. A design must be structured visually, on a per-page basis. The layout must be easy to parse and the content should be organized in such a way as to let the user know what's important and what's ancillary. In addition to organizing a page's content, our designs must make the rest of the site accessible and easy to parse. It should give the user feedback about where they are, what they've just done, and how they can reach the next piece of information or functionality that they want.

I think of it as giving structure to the information that is seen (the visible information on the page) and hidden (all the content not on the current page). Both are equally important, and the best designs find a way to blend the two.

Wireframes

> "With client services, sometimes you need to develop a wireframe that's a deliverable for the client, sometimes you don't. When you don't, sometimes you'll still develop it, but for yourself … I think there shouldn't be one way of doing everything every time."
>
> —Dan Rubin

Alrighty. Now is the time for us to tackle the good stuff.

Wireframes are super-low fidelity (which means simple: lines, boxes, text) designs that focus on content hierarchy, general layout, and functionality. A wireframe should exclude color, texture, or imagery. Instead, it's a purely structural document that tries to organize content and interaction without all the visual clutter that design elements can create. See Figure 4.2 for two wireframe examples from the same project.

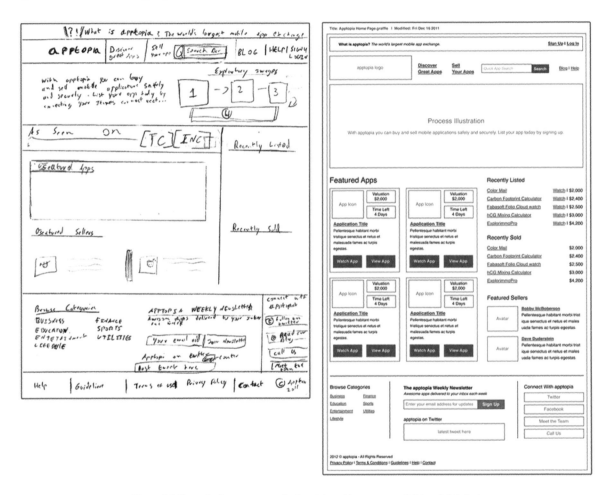

Figure 4.2. Two wireframes, one project: quick and loose versus tight and detailed

In some firms, the UX designer and the interface designer are the same person, but that's not always the case. If you're working in an agency or within a team, the wireframing task will probably fall to another person. Whoever is doing UX will likely hand you a stack of wireframes to work from, so I'd recommend talking candidly with that person to ensure that you receive wireframes of a level of detail that works for you.

How detailed should I make my wireframe?

The level of detail that goes into a wireframe is a subjective decision. The depth of a wireframe often depends on how much of the decision-making process is left to the interface designer and how much is controlled by the UX designer. A detailed wireframe means that the UX designer is already making strong choices about the layout and content hierarchy. Often, wireframes aren't "set in stone" documents, so the interface designer has quite a bit of latitude to move content around when crafting a final mockup.

Wireframe detail can also be affected by the amount of content on a page, or the type of content, as Figure 4.3 proves. A home page with a few lines of text and a couple of big images won't require a detailed wireframe. Because very few elements are on the page, carefully organizing them hierarchically is virtually unnecessary .

Figure 4.3. Wireframes can be as simple or as complex as you wish

By contrast, a home page for a news site with multiple columns of content, featured stories, social media feeds, and video clips will require preplanning. On a busy website like a news site, the wireframe should be given more attention because of the need for structure.

More often than not, the quality of a wireframe is dependent upon how the wireframe is used. In some cases, a wireframe can be used to hammer out very concrete layout and hierarchy decisions. In other cases, the wireframe serves as a general guide for the designer to reference when crafting designs.

Very low-fidelity wireframes can give you plenty of flexibility when designing your layout, but often provide few clues about the details of functionality and the structural necessities of a design. High-fidelity wireframes can provide lots of info about the details of a page, but can make you feel boxed in with your design choices. Your designs don't have to follow the wireframes exactly either, as shown in Figure 4.4.

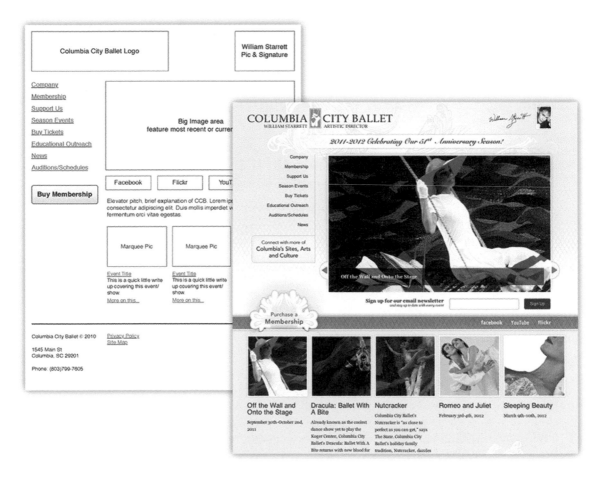

Figure 4.4. Wireframes can be a quick reference for the design elements required and their intended location

Wireframes are a kind of shorthand for final designs. As such, common elements have a simplified representation. Images are represented as a square with lines crossed through it. Forms are boxes with titles over the top line. Horizontal nav elements are long boxes with evenly spaced titles. Text is … well, text. But let me emphasize: nothing fancy! A wireframe can have almost nothing to do with how the final design will look, as Figure 4.5 shows.

Figure 4.5. Use a wireframe loosely if that fits your process

When drafting a wireframe, you should be asking yourself four questions:

- What content needs to be on the page?
- How do the different pieces of content relate to one another?
- How might they possibly be arranged?
- How should the user interact with the content?

That's it. If you're thinking about fonts and imagery, it's likely you're getting ahead of yourself. Just focus on content and structure.

Let's talk a little more in-depth about the ways a wireframe can be used and how to make the most of it for your use case.

Wireframing for Page Layout

Wireframing for page layout is simple, and should feel familiar if you've already been laying out websites. Using the wireframing shorthand, structure the content on the page the way it will appear in the final design. Try to proportion the elements appropriately and focus on creating the underlying structure of the final design. If the wireframe is tight enough, a designer can work on top of it to create the final mockup. Wireframing page layout can also save time by taking the guesswork out of creating the mockup, and shift final layout decisions from the interface team (who makes the mockup) to the UX team (who makes the wireframe).

I usually avoid approaching wireframing from this perspective because I dislike how much it restricts the designer. Additionally, wireframes of this kind tend to be quite detailed and so require more time to craft. Instead, I try to think of wireframes as documents that show *how* to think about the content, a "least is best" approach. If a particular element is grouped with a couple of elements near the top of the page, I take this as a cue that the element is important (because it's near the top of the page) and should appear with these two elements in the final design. That's not to say the element should be in the exact same location as it is in the wireframe. Figure 4.6 shows how I might interpret a wireframe by breaking it into content areas and then deciding on their relative importance.

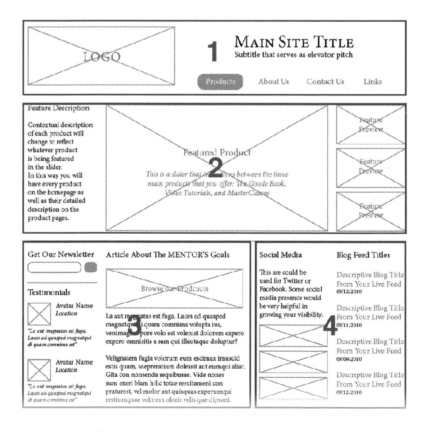

Figure 4.6. Revealing the relative importance of content

A great time to make decisions is during the wireframing process if you're putting together your own wireframes. You can treat the wireframe as a mockup sketch, sort of like a thumbnail. We'll be talking about thumbnails very soon.

Wireframing for Functionality and Interaction

The shorthand used in wireframes accommodates most of the common interactions and elements that make web pages richer than standard text documents. Wireframes can be used to show where buttons belong and video will be placed, and how many elements should be included in the main navigation. In this way, wireframes are perfect for communicating to the designer all the interactions that the user will require. How interactive elements are represented in a wireframe can say a lot about what they actually do, as Figure 4.7 shows.

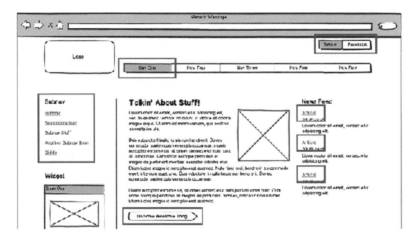

Figure 4.7. Context is key

Because the purpose of wireframes isn't about showing how the final design will look, interactive elements can be laid out as simple line drawings; however, take a little time to think about which interactive elements will be buttons, text links, toggles, sliders, and such. You can give quite a lot of information with simple line drawings.

Wireframing for Content Hierarchy

> "It's important to make sure we're reaching all of our content goals before we start digging into design details."
>
> —Meagan Fisher

When deciding on content hierarchy, a wireframe can be useful because it separates visual design from content. When knocking out a wireframe, skip the fancy stuff like images, fonts, and design elements, indicated in Figure 4.8. In fact, many wireframing tools use Comic Sans as the default font. It sounds awful, but makes sense. Because the font is one that no one (in their right mind) would use for an entire website, I find myself not even thinking about it. I just ignore the font and focus instead on the blocks of text and the image boxes and how they relate to each other.

Figure 4.8. A wireframe is not a design

Content hierarchy is simple to understand in a wireframe, and is determined by just a few factors.

Emphasis of Content by Location

Elements that appear higher on the page tend to be more important. Position indicates prominence in a web page because we can scan pages from top to bottom, and because of "the fold."[1] Content that can only be seen when the user scrolls down the page should, generally speaking, be less important than the content that's immediately viewable when first landing on the page.

Content that is broken off into a sidebar or small column will often be viewed as ancillary or secondary to the main column. It's common for a page's unique content to appear in the main column while content that is repeated from page to page is relegated to the sidebar. This pattern is, in part, due to the way that sites are templated into reusable parts and included in a page. However, it makes good horse sense as well. Compartmentalizing content creates implicit groupings that can be easily scanned, as Figure 4.9 shows.

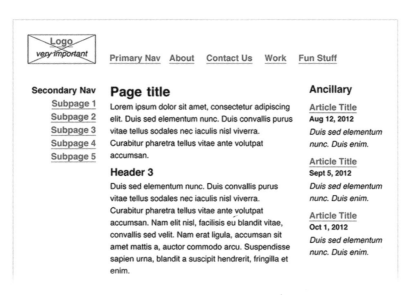

Figure 4.9. In this simple layout, the home link (logo), navigation elements, and content areas are clearly defined and identifiable

---

[1] http://iampaddy.com/lifebelow600/

Emphasis by Size

Visually speaking, elements are put in order of importance by their size. For instance, typographic elements are prioritized by making important text large and standard text small, as Figure 4.10 shows. Content titles are big, but not as big as the page title. Body copy is generally the smallest text, but exceptions are common. Ancillary navigation in the footer might be represented as smaller than body copy size to reduce its footprint. Button labels or image captions might be smaller than body copy because this sort of information could be classified as unnecessary.

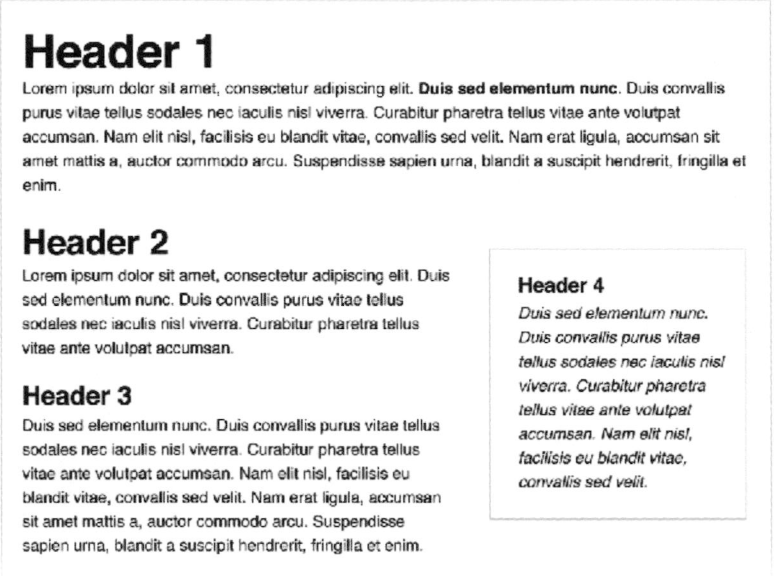

Figure 4.10. Text size plays a significant role in developing a visual hierarchy

Headers play a primary role in ensuring that content has a structured hierarchy. Be consistent when sizing your titles so that users understand the importance of a particular content area. You'd be surprised by the amount of designers who forget this basic rule when it's applied to the Web, as opposed to print design. Avoid falling into that trap. Even though a website is dynamic and inconstant, the typographic structure should be consistent.

Let's remember that elements are not text. Small images floated within the body copy will stand out. A large video element at the top of the page may look insubstantial in a wireframe, but will absolutely dominate a final design. In short, if an element is paramount make it big—at least in the wireframe.

Emphasis by Proximity to Other Elements

This is a little harder to understand, but proximity plays a role in determining the importance of elements. It goes like this: some elements are closely related to other elements, either visually or by content. That relationship can make smaller or less significant elements more prominent because they're visually grouped with other elements, as Figure 4.11 shows.

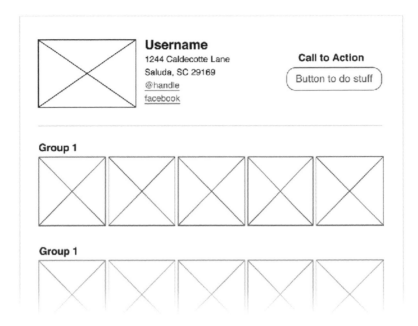

Figure 4.11. Grouping pieces of content logically creates an association between pieces of information

Think about how different pieces of information relate to one another. Those relationships are important, especially if the page has multiple pieces of content. I think that most designers intuitively group content. It's just something that we do when laying out a page, but we should try to be cognizant of the context that we're creating for the page content. If you're wireframing for yourself, you have a head start on thinking about content. If you're wireframing for a client, you can give them more insight into the design being created.

Say that you're designing a profile page with an avatar, a bio, and a full name. It's more than likely that all those elements will be lumped together to form a visual group. That group then becomes the visual element that's prioritized in the wireframe. All the elements in the group then have to be organized within the visual hierarchy of the entire layout, as well as within the group they form.

You can say a lot about the content of a page by how you group the elements. Taking the time to think about how the different pieces of content relate to one another can make a huge difference in readability and overall accessibility.

Wireframing Tools

I'm not going to go nuts talking about the various wireframing tools available, but I will say that a number of them are high quality, and some happen to be free.

I used to make wireframes in Adobe Illustrator. I created a number of symbols that were wireframing elements, which worked quite well, but any element with text was a pain to edit or update. When I decided to seek out a dedicated wireframing tool, I looked at two options:

Pencil Project (http://www.evolus.vn/Pencil/Home.html)
This is free and can run either as a Firefox add-on or as a stand-alone desktop app. It's fairly full-featured, but a little clunky to use. Still, did I mention it's free?

Balsamiq (http://www.balsamiq.com/)
This is a more robust wireframing tool that's very easy to use. It also can be used in the browser or as a desktop app, but costs $79.

It's up to you how you put your wireframes together, whether it's in Illustrator, with a pencil, or with a dedicated wireframing tool. What's important is that you understand how they're crafted and what they're used for. If you put enough time and thought into your wireframes, you'll find that even the simplest one can help bridge the gap between thinking about how a site will work and crafting the final design.

Thumbnails

> "Usually we'll start … with a planning stage, where we'll sit down and start sketching, because we've found that paper is probably the easiest way to get your ideas out … [Ideas] can also be trash, so you can literally crumple up an idea and get rid of it."
>
> —Dave Rupert

If you've never sketched a **thumbnail**, it's a small drawing of a design—as seen in Figure 4.12—that's usually no more than a couple of inches square. Thumbnails can be drawn speedily and serve as a shorthand for design ideas. Most of the time, thumbnails are used to sketch out the overall structure of a design, but they can also be used to iterate on individual parts of a design. Thumbnails that are only a portion of a design are called **details**.

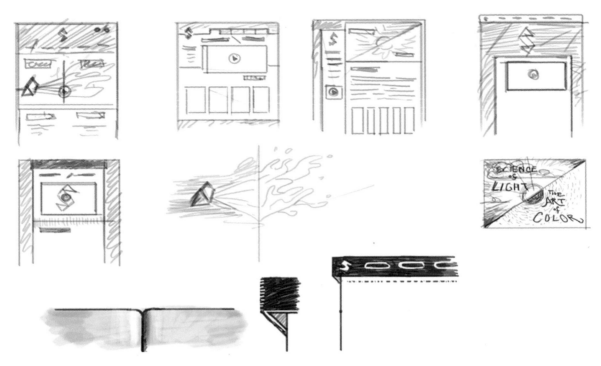

Figure 4.12. Thumbnails and details allow us to iterate through design ideas quickly

A Case for Sketching

> "I am a great believer in thumbnail sketches … lots of rapid iteration in a short
> amount of time … Anything that is very efficient at the 'brain dump,' I love. So …
> quick sketches, tiny little one-inch sketches, I love, because you can bash out twenty
> or thirty of them in a five-minute span. It's visual brainstorming."
>
> —Dan Rubin

When I was a teacher, getting students to draw thumbnails was akin to pulling teeth. They were so eager to jump into their designs that they wanted to skip over this part of the process. Maybe they failed to see the value of sketching and thumbnailing. Whatever the reason, sketching out ideas is a good habit to have and I encourage it whenever possible.

I'm a big advocate for drawing on a daily basis, so here are a few reasons why you should add sketching to your workflow.

Slow Down, It's Not a Race!

Sketching slows us down and gives us a few more minutes to think about each idea. Certainly, thumbnails are fast to draw, but internal thoughts are much faster *and less distinct*. By taking the time to sketch out each idea in a thumbnail drawing, we are forced to consider not only the details of the design, but also whether or not it will really look good as a whole.

I know that time is money, but so is quality. Give yourself a little time to jot down your ideas. Doing so doesn't take long, and the benefits far outweigh the costs.

Do It for Everyone Else

Sketching creates a record of our ideas that can be shared with our peers. If we're unsure which design to choose, we can throw it to another designer, who will look at it with unbiased eyes.

I've found that other people see my designs in ways that I'm unable to. If I show them iterations of thumbnails or rough designs, they can pick out the good parts and slash through the bad. Even better, they do it fast. I might sit at my desk for an hour agonizing over a few sketches, because I can't decide which, if any, is actually good. If one of my friends comes over, they'll tell me what they think within seconds of looking.

We need these snap judgments because that's the kind of decision that both clients and users will make. They don't know what we were *trying to achieve* with our designs. They see the design for what it is, not always what we want it to be.

Face It, Your First Idea Is Usually the Worst

Seriously, our first ideas tend to be boring and boilerplate, but it's important to work through them. Iterating over pedestrian ideas gives us time to develop a clearer sense of what we're designing and to find opportunities for something special.

You might find yourself putting the finishing touches on a design and thinking, "It ain't great, but it's done and I'm not doing it again. Ship it!" Charming colloquialisms notwithstanding, you should probably consider thumbnailing for your next project.

You Won't Get Emotional

Sketching allows us to work through our least interesting ideas quickly, with little commitment to a finished design. I can hammer through a dozen crappy thumbnails in less than an hour. Because sketching thumbnails is so fast, I can keep going until I work out two or three novel sketches that might make good final mockups.

> "I usually start on a whiteboard or a piece of paper. I'm a terrible draftsman, but I can at least sketch down ... bits of information that we want to display. Are they the right bits of information? What order do we want to display them in? What do we emphasize? We'll work on that kind of visual hierarchy and basically decide 'What are our requirements?'"
>
> —Daniel Burka

When I skip thumbnailing and jump into Photoshop to iterate over an idea, I find myself growing attached to particular elements or design choices. I want to keep aspects from one design in the next. I agonize over minute details when I should be focused on producing as many different designs as possible. In short, I become attached to the designs because they require a lot of me, and I lose sight of the fact that *I'm just trying out ideas*, not polishing up a mockup. That's bad mojo.

Throwaway drawings are an excellent way to hammer out a wide range of ideas quickly. I rarely find myself emotionally attached to a two-inch pencil thumbnail that took four minutes to draw. On many levels, that's a good thing …

Sketches aren't supposed to be works of art. In fact, you may never show them to a client. You may never show them to your peers. Most of the time, I only show the few that I like to other designers. I may have pages of garbage ideas that never again see the light of day.

Don't get hung up on the details, and never scrimp on the sketching.

Grayboxing

Grayboxing is a fairly simple concept, so I will avoid spending too much time on it. It involves producing a design that's halfway between a wireframe and a full mockup. It's informed by the thumbnail sketches, and is far more detailed than a simple wireframe. You still won't be adding elements like color, texture, or imagery, but you do start refining the layout, working on the distribution of values and typography.

To create a graybox, start with your thumbnail. Scale the thumbnail to a full-sized design and block in the major shapes and elements. Add real content in the form of typography and develop the typographic treatment. Pick real fonts and think deeply about the typographic hierarchy. This is less about employing imagery or graphics, and more about adding borderlines, shapes, and grayscale values.

Grayboxing, illustrated in Figure 4.13, is similar to how the Old Masters used to paint. Many Renaissance painters employed a method of painting called "grisaille," a French word that translates to "gray." The method basically works by progressing through a few well-defined stages.

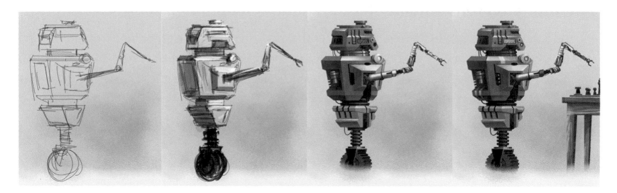

Figure 4.13. The grisaille method of painting

First, the artist would sketch their chosen composition on the canvas. The canvas was painted white or a shade of gray. Then, in thin layers of oil paint, the painting was built with shades of gray ranging from solid black to pure white. The result was a grayscale rendering of whatever the artist was painting. Imagine a charcoal drawing, only with oil paint.

After the painting was completed in grays, the artist would paint colors on top of the grayscale image, applying very thin layers of paint. Textural treatments and detailed work were left for last. The result would be a painting of deep values and rich color.

Many Old Master painters employed this method because of the consistent quality it produced and the structured methodology. Grisaille is a highly refined process that requires a multitude of skills, but can produce spectacular, luminous results. By working the art up layer by layer, an artist is able to achieve a visual depth that other methods cannot.

I think that as we develop our web design process, we search for ways to refine our understanding of each stage. Wireframing is the step that allows us to focus on content and hierarchy. Thumbnailing forces us to look at the layout as a whole instead of as a collection of discreet components. We are impelled to think about the look in broad strokes.

Grayboxing combines the macro views that we gain from wireframes and thumbnails. Before we focus on the minutiae of texture, color, and style (in the final mockup), we take the step to create a layout that is focused on value, structure, typography, and elegance. A grayboxed design should be concise and functional. It should have everything in place to be useful and cohesive. It's design without all the sizzle, but it is fundamental.

Only after we've built a design that is tight and functional, do we paint on those last layers of color. Only in the final hour do we layer on the texture, the splashes of imagery, and the tight little patterns that we all seem to love so much. When you are grayboxing, the little details are just the icing on the cake. The graybox is where you determine most of the functional design.

When is grayboxing useful?

Some designers consider grayboxing to be a superfluous step towards a great mockup, and in some cases I agree. If you have a very clear vision of what you want to achieve with your design, grayboxing might be an unnecessary step; however, if you want to build your design at a structured pace and let the look and feel develop over time, grayboxing might really help you tighten up a design.

In the end, you have a grayscale design that closely resembles what you want your final design to look like, but without all the shiny bits.

The Problem with Templates and Why You'll Still Use Them

As interactive designers, part of our job is to understand the entire structure of our site and create an interface that accommodates that structure. Websites that use templates might require each major area of our layout to be modular and reusable. It's just a necessity of the way websites are built.

Say, for instance, we are building a site for a home builder. Let's call this home building company HomeConstructors Inc. (I hope you appreciate my creativity). As per HomeConstructors's request, we craft a home page that shows off the newest floor plans. We make pages that list its available floor plans, employee biographies, company history, and contact details. HomeConstructors love it, and all is well with the world.

Two weeks later, the president of HomeConstructors decides she wants a blog and event calendar. We are jazzed about the extra work when we suddenly realize that we now have to shoehorn functionality into a site that we didn't anticipate. It will be necessary to make compromises to the content to fit the design. This may sound like small potatoes to many of you, but it is a big deal. A design should be crafted to accommodate and accentuate the content, rather than the other way around.

Consider this example: You build a site for the local theater group but find that after you've finished, they create a page featuring 300 photos that completely breaks the layout, making you look like an amateur. Some matters are unavoidable, but we can do our best to head off any potential problems. You might be able to anticipate the need for a gallery on the site, in which case you'll go ahead and create a specific gallery template.

If you're building a site that won't be content managed or only has a few pages, you might have a little more latitude with how pages are laid out; in my experience, however, most clients lack the expertise to hack their own websites. Raw HTML is almost always dropped in favor of dynamic content and some kind of management system.

Overcoming the Problem

I don't think dynamic systems are a problem, but using them means we have to build sites that can accommodate pages and functionality that was unanticipated. The fact of the matter is that most of the sites you design will be managed somehow, so embrace the idea of designing with flexibility. It can save you a lot of headaches.

To mitigate the problem, I usually design a minimum of two layouts, but often more. Custom pages are easy to identify because they usually feature specific or unique functionality. Just think, a site that you build for a hospital will have features and functionality that differ greatly from the site you build for HomeConstructors. Can you think of what those differences might be?

While you're contemplating that situation, I'll show you how I think about designing pages.

The Home Page

This page often receives the bulk of our attention, even though most users spend much of their time on internal pages. Sure, it depends on the site, but generally speaking if users don't proceed past your home page, they miss most of the site. Figure 4.14 shows a home page wireframe that's simple, but covers all the bases.

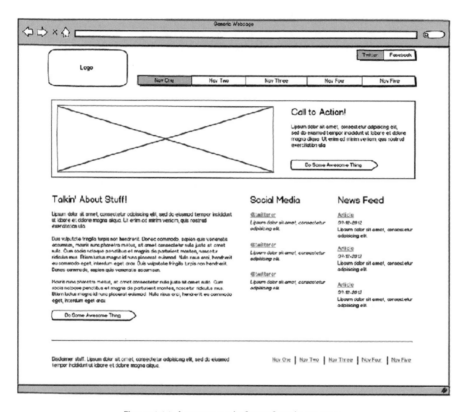

Figure 4.14. A common wireframe for a home page

I've also found that the home page tends to be the most unique and malleable of all web pages. Sometimes, I save the design of this page for last because of its lack of flexibility. I'd rather circumvent design choices that translate poorly to other pages on the site, so I might save the home page until much of the utilitarian design has been completed.

A Generic Subpage

It's not sexy, but you're going to need a template design to handle most of the usual stuff. I try to design a generic subpage that can accommodate a sidebar, secondary navigation, breadcrumbs, and possibly some sort of content feed. Sometimes the sidebar is the same element as the secondary nav. The content feed should be able to serve as a news feed, events feed, or blog feed. You've likely seen thousands of website subpages structured in the way shown in Figure 4.15.

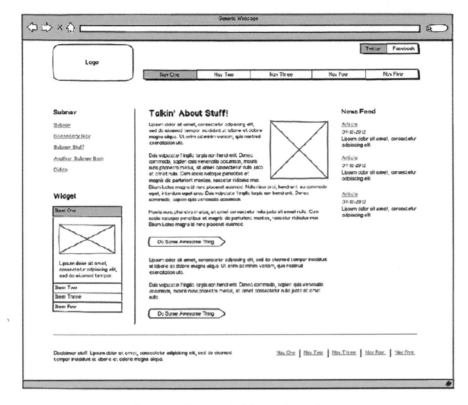

Figure 4.15. Your standard three-column subpage

What's important about this design is that it should work with any combination of elements—or none. If the page needs breadcrumbs and a secondary nav, it should be easy enough. The same goes for a news feed and sidebar. Keep in mind that each of these elements is independent of the page's primary content, the latter which you may be unable to control.

The point is that this design is your attempt to create a blank slate that can handle any content. It'll go a long way, but will eventually fail you on some level because more often than not, a single subpage template isn't enough. You'll need special pages for special content.

Our subpage design is fine for informational content; it might even serve well as a profile page or an admin section. We can keep the structure, but include different content to handle similar pages; however, it will only work some of the time. What if the site has some special functionality, some feature that requires the whole page to be a single column and excludes the news feed? Maybe you need to have form pages that have nothing but the form fields and explanatory text on them? What if the site has an interactive game, or an internal app for manipulating data? All these cases call for special pages and special functionality.

To deal with these pages, we need special templates.

The Specialized Subpage

You'll probably have pages that feature unique content and functionality. These pages will require their own design, at least in part. Often, by stripping the generic subpage of all possible elements, you'll have a good open layout to incorporate the specialized content for pages like the one in Figure 4.16. And don't be afraid to wireframe additional layouts.

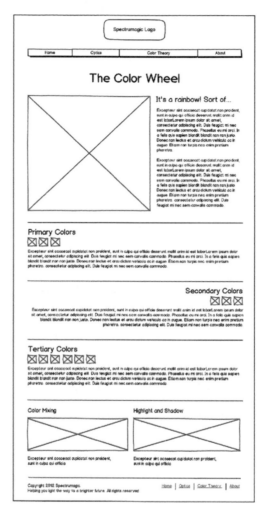

Figure 4.16. You'll need to break the mold for pages with special content

Forms often need special templates because of their additional functionality. Forms are also tedious for users, so removing as many extraneous links as possible is a good idea. That means removing the sidebar and news feed, maybe even the main navigation. Creating a basic form with fewer options simplifies the user experience, as illustrated in Figure 4.17.

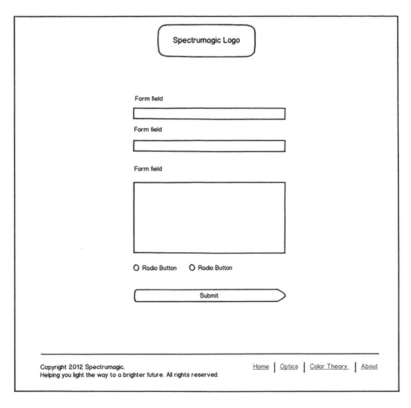

Figure 4.17. Stripping down the page layout aids user focus

As long as the look and feel of each page is unified, the varied layouts shouldn't detract from the user's experience. If everything is easy to understand, if they can find what they're looking for and accomplish their goals quickly, the user won't give it a second thought, and that's what you want.

Designing for Multiple Form Factors

The days of designing fixed-width 960-pixel-wide websites are behind us. The markets for smartphones, tablet devices, and personal computers have created an environment where websites need to function on vastly different screen sizes and form factors, as Figure 4.18 illustrates. Desktop monitors can be over 2,000 pixels wide, while some phones are less than 400 pixels.

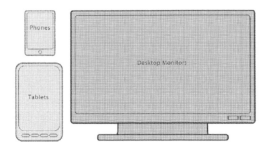

Figure 4.18. It's a tall order making sites that look good on all devices, but it's the future, so get used to it

Now, high-pixel-density displays, like the iPad's retina display (which has a higher resolution than most desktop monitors) are complicating the problem even further. The first- and second-generation iPads had a resolution of 1024px × 768px. The third generation iPad is the same size, but its resolution is 2048px × 1536px. It leaves us with two devices that have almost exactly the same physical dimensions, but drastically different resolutions.

Variations in pixel density, size, and form factor have forced the industry to reevaluate how a website should be experienced. Couple that with different operating systems and multiple browsers, and we have a potential nightmare. We need solutions to present users with good experiences, no matter what device they're using. I'm now going to introduce a couple of common solutions to this problem and briefly discuss their pros and cons.

Mobile Sites

A mobile site is built specifically for a mobile device, but with the aim of reflecting a desktop site of the same content. When a user goes to the site on their desktop computer, they are routed to the version of the site that works best for their desktop monitor. Similarly, if a user visits the site on their phone, they will be directed to the mobile version of the site that has been specifically optimized for small devices. Figure 4.19 shows an example of a company site on two separate devices.

Figure 4.19. Sometimes the experiences provided for different devices require a separate website entirely

It's a fairly straightforward approach: If you need a site that works on both the desktop and smartphone, make two sites. Any visitor to the site will be routed to the version that works best on their device.

Taking this approach involves a number of technical hurdles, though. For instance, how do we accurately detect which device is displaying the site? How do we maintain the same content on two separate websites? What do we do for tablet computers or notebook computers?

Granted, all these problems have solutions, but it's worth noting that designing two sites that are supposed to act as one adds layers of complexity that would otherwise not exist.

Pros

For the most part, mobile sites have fallen out of favor, but I still think they have their place. If the experience that your desktop site provides differs significantly from the experience that you want users to have on their phone, a mobile site is probably a good choice. Because they can both be designed independently, from the ground up, special considerations can be made for each site that have nothing to do with the other.

I think that mobile sites have a place with web apps. High levels of interaction and functionality can be hard to translate from a large desktop version to a tiny handheld device.

On a desktop computer, a web app can be laid out in multiple panels. Some areas can show readouts of information, while others have controls for manipulating that information. Data can be pulled on the fly using Ajax, so the whole app might be one page. On a small device, each part of the app (the readouts, the controls, and so on) might need to be on separate pages. The entire structure of the app may be completely different, even though the content is the same. Because of the wide variance in how the two sites need to be built, a mobile version might be the most appropriate.

Cons

In a word: *duplication.*

If you build two sites, everything has to be done twice. Sure, both sites can pull from the same databases; I'll bet they'd even share a great deal of server-side code, but everything else has to be done twice. All the UX work, design work, and front-end development is automatically duplicated. Duplication means time and money.

The other issue with a mobile site is that "mobile" is more than just one device. As we talked about at the beginning of this section, we have to accommodate dozens of sizes, resolutions, and form factors. Are we supposed to build a site for each possible device?

Mobile sites are an attempt to give users a rewarding experience no matter how they access the site or what device they own. Providing a site for each possibility is next to impossible.

Responsive Design

So, the question becomes: "If I want to avoid duplicating my efforts, and it's unnecessary to provide completely different experiences for the user, how do I build sites that work on all devices?"

These days, the answer is **responsive web design**. A couple of years ago, Ethan Marcotte wrote an article for *A List Apart* about something he called responsive web design.[2] Rather than go over the details here, I'd suggest you give it a read.

I will, however, explain how responsive design works in simple terms. As I mentioned before, we aren't concerned with the details of implementing a responsive design at this time, but because we need to know *how responsive design affects our process*, it's important to understand how it works.

> "If I'm working on a responsive design … before I begin … [I] figure out how it's going to adapt to different screen sizes."
>
> —Meagan Fisher

Responsive design is a method of combining **fluid layouts** (which shrink and grow as a browser is resized) with **media queries** (CSS conditional statements that apply styles if certain conditions are met) to produce a site that can shift and change depending on the browser window's resolution.

For instance, a media query can check to see if the maximum width of the viewport is less than 480px, and if so, the style will be applied. If the viewport is greater than 480px wide, the style won't be. Media queries can also be used to detect if the device is in landscape or portrait orientation, as well as other qualities, giving us tight control over when styles are applied and how.

Each media query creates a breakpoint, where the fluid layout will change based upon the new styles for that resolution. A **breakpoint** is the point when the next media query resolves true and new styles are applied to the design. Responsive designs allow us to create websites that change to best suit the pixel dimensions of all devices, as shown in Figure 4.20.

Pros

Responsive design is completely resolution-independent. It's easy enough to do, in a technical sense, and it allows for one codebase across all devices. We only need one stylesheet and an HTML document to create a responsive layout in almost all modern browsers.

---

[2] www.alistapart.com/articles/responsive-web-design

Figure 4.20. A responsive design suited to 350px, 500px, 800px, and 1200px screens

Instead of focusing on the many resolutions of each mobile device, we can create breakpoints for our content and design. We can look for the places where the fluid layout starts to break down, and create breakpoints to handle the transitions between differing page widths. Figure 4.21 shows how as a responsive site becomes wider, the media queries trigger and adjust the layout to best support the content. Nifty.

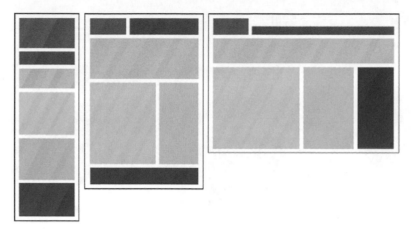

Figure 4.21. A responsive site responding to changing conditions

Finally, and I think most importantly, responsive design forces us to consider almost exclusively the presentation of our content. We have to focus on structuring our content, so that responsive design is possible. We are obligated to think about how our content will appear on a huge range of devices: How will we show content on a mobile phone that fills a desktop monitor? If we have to cut down on content, what will we want to display on the phone? If certain content is unsuitable for the phone, should we display it on the website?

All these questions are great! We should have been asking them all along.

Cons

Honestly, I'm hard-pressed to identify many problems with responsive design. As I mentioned before, media queries have no support in older browsers, but we have multiple workarounds at our disposal. Still, a couple of sticking points do matter when adapting your workflow to accommodate responsive design.

The first sticky wicket is that responsive design requires a change in approach for designing a website. Because the design has to adapt to multiple form factors and resolutions, we're required to give more consideration to markup. How do we design a site that can function well on a 400-pixels-wide smartphone yet can scale to 2,000 pixels without a hitch? It's simple enough, but it does take a willingness to embrace the dynamic nature of content and quite a bit more forethought.

With static-width layouts, only when the design is complete do I even think about markup, because I know that I can mark up just about anything in a semantic way. I just design what I want and worry about the markup later. However, taking such a gung-ho approach with responsive design is not recommended; otherwise you might find that you have to spend more time wireframing the breakpoints in your designs in order to write clean, semantic HTML and CSS.

Want to get your hands dirty?

A deep technical discussion on how to implement mobile sites and responsive design is beyond the scope of this book. I merely wanted to introduce these approaches for handling the presentation of websites across multiple devices. If you want to learn more, here are some great resources:

- Ethan Marcotte's Book (http://www.abookapart.com/products/responsive-web-design/)

- An awesome visual representation of responsive design (http://www.thismanslife.co.uk/projects/lab/responsiveillustration/)

- The article that started it all (http://www.alistapart.com/articles/responsive-web-design/)

- Responsive `min-width` based media queries (http://unmatchedstyle.com/news/working-with-media-queries-and-min-width.php)

Don't Sweat the Small Stuff

All this work before you even start designing might seem overkill, but I encourage you to try it out. You'll see that taking a couple of extra steps to organize your ideas and understand the problems that you're solving will serve you well when putting together your designs. No need to get hung up on following a strict procedure of wireframes, thumbnails, grayboxes, and design. Think of each of these steps as a tool.

Wireframes help you control and understand a site's content and interactions. Thumbnails help you iterate through design ideas quickly without being sidetracked by small details. Grayboxes are an intermediate step between thumbnails and a full design. They help you to focus your attention on typography, content, and value.

So, don't sweat the small stuff. I think Dan Rubin did a good job of putting it into words:

> "I'd get bored if I had one process, but all these tools [wireframing, brainstorming, and thumbnail sketching] are useful, no matter what your process is, so long as you know when to use them."
>
> —Dan Rubin

In the next chapter, we'll *really* design something, I promise. We've talked a lot about how to collect information and plan for a design, and I've done all of that for our Spectrumagic site. Let's take a look at that work and see how it informs our final mockup.

Chapter 5

Design Patterns: Tried and Trusted Solutions

In 1994, a group of developers wrote a book called *Design Patterns: Elements of Reusable Object-Oriented Software* (Boston: Addison-Wesley, 1994),[1] wherein they explored the pros and cons of object-oriented software engineering. This group of developers, commonly referred to as "The Gang of Four" or "GoF," identified common software engineering problems and how object-oriented programming (OOP) could be used to solve those problems. The book refers to these solutions as **design patterns**, some of which can be seen in Figure 5.1.

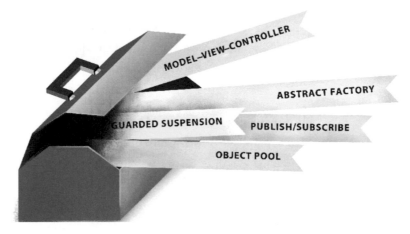

Figure 5.1. Engineering design patterns are a big part of the developer's toolbox

[1] http://www.pearsonhighered.com/pearsonhigheredus/educator/product/products_detail.page?isbn=0201633612

The idea behind the book is that every software engineer faces the same standard problems in most of their projects:

- How do we read and write information to files and databases in a sensible way?

- How do we validate that data intelligently and securely?

- How do we structure our software so that the data model and the visual representation of that data are independent of one another? (more on that shortly)

- How do we design for future extensions that might be added to the system?

Those are just a few example questions that an engineer might ask on any given project, regardless of the size.

Over time, developers create their own homegrown solutions to problems. They might write a small library of code or a set of reusable snippets that provide the functionality they want. Eventually, they end up with a collection of code that can be reused on a daily basis. It's faster, and saves them from reinventing the wheel for every project. This approach is well and good for a developer, but it does create a few hairy situations.

The main problem—and one that will offend many egos—is that most developers, myself included, sometimes miss the mark when trying to create perfect solutions the first time around on a project. The code we write might have logical flaws or lack the flexibility that we could need later, requiring massive rewrites. As we are faced with more complex development tasks, we're forced to plan in greater detail. This need for detail and structure requires that all our designs accommodate the possibility of change and growth.

In very basic terms, any problem that we need to invent a solution for is, by definition, one that currently has no solution. The GoF's design patterns are intended to address most possible scenarios by providing tried-and-tested remedies to avoid producing further issues that our homegrown solutions might.

If a developer needs to create separation between the visual representation of their interface and the data that exists in the back end, the **Model–View–Controller (MVC) pattern** is designed to do just that. It can be seen in Figure 5.2.

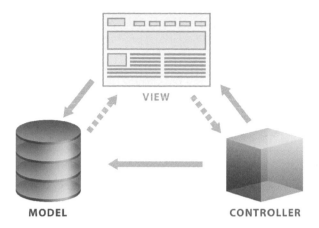

Figure 5.2. The MVC pattern separates the interface code from the controller code and model code

The MVC pattern is designed to separate the code that handles all layers of an application. The view manages all the code that updates the visual interface of the design. It accepts input from the user via the controller and communicates with it. The controller code sends messages back and forth with the model and tells the view when and how to update itself. Finally, the model code handles all the data and business logic on the back end.

When code is separated in this way, it's easier to understand and update. Plus, the functionality is segmented and helps to avoid the dreaded "spaghetti code." It also allows the flexibility to present data on another interface if necessary just by switching out the views.

By reducing software engineering challenges to their fundamental components, the GoF have created a common language and approach to solving those problems. The GoF's design patterns also help to enforce best practices in the industry. A common set of solutions that are bulletproof and future-proof means that software is fairly easy to edit and extend, even if the codebase is built by another developer. A developer who is familiar with OOP and design patterns can look at a system and, with relative ease, understand how it works and how to change it.

How does this relate to web design?

When proposing their design patterns, the GoF were trying to standardize how developers approach problem solving. They were also documenting best practices and quality solutions that could simplify a developer's workflow and ease the complexities of communicating a cobbled or unique API. Design patterns give developers the common language and structure needed to create compatible and supportable software. Web designers may have their own toolbox of design patterns, as shown in Figure 5.3.

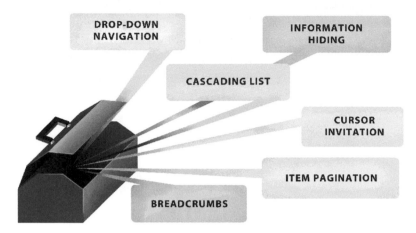

Figure 5.3. Knowing web design patterns can make a big difference in your process

Although they differ from those solved by the GoF, web designers also face a large set of common problems on a daily basis. Web designs need to communicate content and craft intuitive interactions. This criteria can create potential problems for any project, regardless of the size:

- How will users navigate our site?
- How should the content be structured so that it's easy to parse through?
- What content is most important and how will that be communicated?
- How will the design change for different devices, resolutions, and form factors?
- How do we want users to utilize the home page?
- How will the design communicate different interactions?
- How will the design accommodate dynamic content?
- How do we communicate the main objectives of the site?

And so on.

Clearly, we're faced with a lot more questions than these to create a quality and usable design, but this should give you a fair idea of what I mean. In one form or another, it's probable you've asked yourself questions like these for every design you've ever executed. Wouldn't it be helpful if there was a list of standard solutions our users understood that we could utilize to create compelling designs?

Am I ripping people off?

Web design is highly complex and requires a great deal of understanding of multiple disciplines. Learning all these disciplines can be difficult for most designers and next to impossible for some. Luckily, we have a vibrant community of very smart people who've made it their mission to focus on specific parts of the web design process. Those people have given us a wealth of knowledge from which to draw whenever we are coming up short.

Design patterns have been developed through years of trial and error. The solutions in most pattern libraries are solid ideas for how to communicate interaction and intent to a user. I've discussed this with a number of designers who are concerned that adopting design patterns limits their creativity and forces them to make designs that look like everyone else's. Don't confuse design patterns with visual style. Design patterns are fundamentally more abstract than style and can accommodate any look or feel.

Think about horizontal navigation. You've probably laid out dozens of horizontal navs and they all look different, because they're styled to suit the context of the whole page. Every horizontal nav is still a horizontal nav, right? Even though one has textures and bright colors, it's still fundamentally the same as one that is minimal and achromatic; consider Figure 5.4.

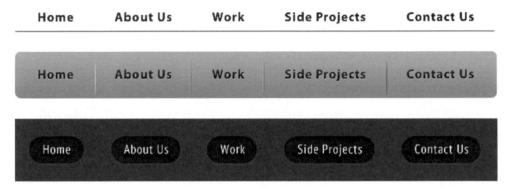

Figure 5.4. Every horizontal navigation bar follows the same design pattern, no matter how it looks

A design pattern is the configuration of elements, not the way those elements look. If you take a series of links to other pages and display them inline at the top of a page, you've created a horizontal nav. Period. Adopting design patterns as a way to standardize page layout and element design doesn't restrict our freedom as designers.

I have no objection to creative expression, quite the contrary. I encourage everyone to explore new ideas and learn from that exploration. However, design patterns exist because they are proven. Not every part of a design needs to be reinvented for each design. Sure, the look and feel can be different. Go nuts with design elements; that's the fun part! Just don't forget that every choice you make needs to be visually attractive and functional. Design patterns inform the functional aspect of the design process.

> "I try to get to the simplest solution first … I'll strip [the problem] down to nothing. Sometimes, I'll even close the project. I'll get out of all the design, all the code, and … I'll open a new file. I'll build a reduced version of the problem I'm having and try to find the simplest elegant solution."
>
> —Dave Rupert

Dave is Lead Developer at Paravel,[2] and while he is talking about front-end, dev-related problems and solutions, I think that he gets to the heart of design patterns with his comment. He strips away everything unrelated to the subject at hand, so that he can see the root problem clearly. He even goes so far as to create isolated and reduced versions of the issue so that he can solve it in a vacuum.

This is exactly what a design pattern does. Design patterns are solutions to isolated but common problems. They banish concerns about visual design and style, identify the root of a problem, and propose a solid, workable solution that does the job 99% of the time.

No one is going to hold your feet to the fire and make you memorize design patterns and the theory behind them. Rather than memorize them, I just treat them as guides when I run across problems that I'm unable to effectively solve on my own.

Types of Design Patterns

Most designers work intuitively, putting content on the page where it "feels right" and makes sense. Often, while designing, we are employing patterns without realizing it. But it's essential that we understand the patterns on a deep and fundamental level, otherwise we'll only be able to fully utilize the most basic structural patterns in our designs.

> "I think I have trouble abstracting things. I tend to go straight to a straight solution. Once I get an idea … I'll just throw myself at that … I tend to rush towards the final solution faster than I should and then double back and figure out why that didn't work."
>
> —Shaun Inman

I'd imagine quite a few designers have the same approach as Shaun, wanting to reach the finish line as fast as possible, but that requires knowing how to get there. Design patterns can help us quickly fill in the gaps for how to approach a problem. Because design patterns are tested and focused, we know that by understanding them, our solutions will work and makes sense.

Extolling the virtues of design patterns is far from saying that all our designs should look the same. Personally, I like to think of patterns by what they accomplish, rather than in terms of how they look. For instance, drop-down menus are often cited as a common navigation pattern. While I agree that they're common, I think that drop-down menus are actually a combination of two fundamental patterns, identified in Figure 5.5.

---

[2] http://paravelinc.com

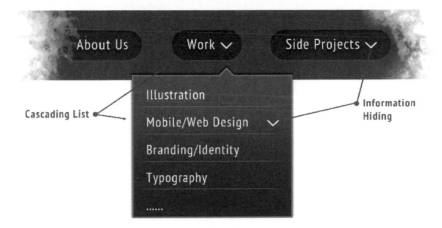

Figure 5.5. A drop-down is the combination of the Cascading List and Information Hiding

The first is an information pattern called a **Cascading List**. Cascading Lists are designed to help users parse through a deep tree structure of information where categories (or pages) have subcategories, and those subcategories have sub-subcategories, and so forth.

With a drop-down, the user either clicks or hovers over a link within the primary navigation. The hovered link expands to reveal a sublisting of all the pages that are its direct children. Sometimes, these sublistings might expand to reveal their children. This pattern allows users to drill down from a broad category to something more specific. Drop-downs can have multiple levels to quickly move through a deep site architecture, but I wouldn't recommend it. For example, Figure 5.6 goes from "Awesome Site!" to reveal "Work" and "Branding" menu options.

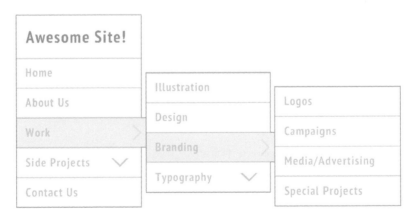

Figure 5.6. Drop-downs with too many levels

The second pattern employed by drop-down navigation is called **Information Hiding**, where ancillary or secondary information is hidden from the user until such time as they actually need it. The idea is that primary navigation creates a broad overview of the site and breaks the content into discrete areas of concentration or functionality. If the user clicks on one of the main navigation links, they'll be transported to the content within that area of the site. Once there, they are presented with more links to narrower fields of interest within the main area. And so forth and so on.

A drop-down menu combines a Cascading List and Information Hiding to create a visual and interactive solution to a user's need to parse large blocks of nested content. A drop-down also keeps the list's footprint small.

Another example of Information Hiding is when designers put content in a **modal window**—a child window in the web page that requires further user interaction to return to the page. On many marketing sites, the home page will often have small cards, as highlighted in blue in Figure 5.7. The cards are small sections containing snippets of information that are designed to entice you to click on them. When clicked, the cards will open to a page or modal window with more detailed content.

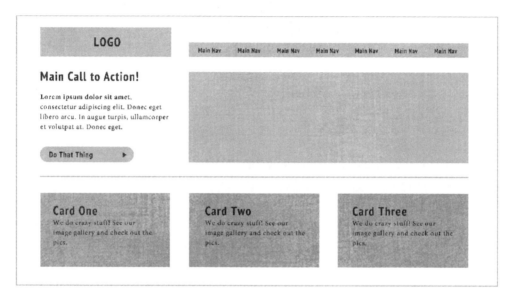

Figure 5.7. The blue cards clearly lead to some sort of content, which is hidden from the user until they click through the link

In a scenario such as this, the designer has chosen to hide the content behind an interaction. Instead of placing content on the home page, they design a link that leads to the content. Sometimes this is a great decision, and sometimes it isn't. The point is that the content was intentionally hidden behind an interaction.

A quick web search for UI design patterns will reveal many design pattern libraries. Some of the patterns are well documented and appear on a lot of sites, but most are a reflection of the author of the libraries' opinions. Instead of creating an exhaustive list of patterns for you to memorize, I'm going to show you how I see patterns and the problems that they help to solve.

In general, UI design patterns:

- help users to create a mental model of the content and interaction[3]
- provide solid solutions to common problems faced by web designers

---

[3] Donald Norman pioneered mental models in user-centered design (http://www.jnd.org/dn.mss/design_as_communication.html)

I think that all patterns can be put into one of five categories. Much like the drop-down menu that we just talked about, the design choices we make are often combinations of patterns that provide the visual solutions we need for our problems.

I'm going to briefly discuss these categories and give a couple of examples of each. This is a very broad overview, but my hope is that when designing your next site, you'll have a greater sense of the problems you are trying to solve with your design. By better understanding the issues that underpin your design problems and how design patterns solve them, we can produce results that are more intuitive and logically structured for our users.

Visual Patterns

Broadly speaking, visual design patterns are those that deal with how our design looks. You might interpret this to mean that visual design patterns deal only with the superficial visual layer of a design, but that's not entirely true.

In many ways, visual patterns are the same as patterns in all visual design. Color patterns, the principles and elements of design, and Gestalt theory[4] are all sources of visual patterns, but a few are specific to interactive design.

First of all, visual patterns communicate a wide range of information to the user. They create context and hierarchy for our content, and communicate to the user what actions they can take at any given point. They create the mood and character of a design, and help to build trust between the site and the user.

> "We underestimate the power of emotions. Even executives, who like to see numbers, really make their decisions on emotions."
>
> —Donald Norman

We should never disregard the emotional impact our designs have on a user. Certainly, we want to avoid creating any glaring usability problems when designing a site, but there will always be issues. Yet, if you can inspire trust and love through visual design, you can go a long way towards encouraging the user to forgive any of the design's shortcomings.

We love to wax on about the technical aspects of our designs, but emotion is just as important. Visuals and imagery are the major vehicles for emotion.

Layout Patterns

Layout patterns are used in the arrangement of content on the page. Location matters a great deal in design. Layout patterns are common configurations and structures that make a design familiar and navigable for a wide range of users.

---

[4] http://graphicdesign.spokanefalls.edu/tutorials/process/gestaltprinciples/gestaltprinc.htm

Think of almost any website. You probably see a site like the one shown in Figure 5.8, with some sort of header section at the top of the page, main navigation, a prominent logo, and possibly links to ancillary content like social media, blogs, or other affiliate sites.

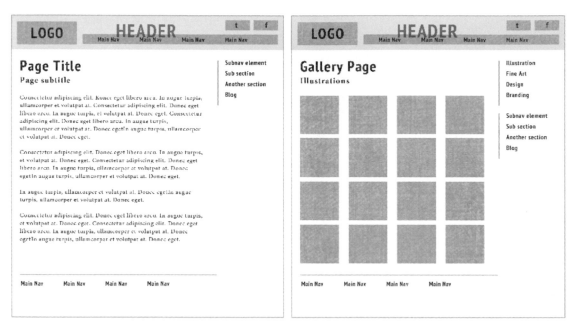

Figure 5.8. Site headers with a logo, main navigation bar, and social media links appear on almost every site on the Internet

Below that, there's an area for the page's content. The area will likely have two or three columns. The widest column will contain the primary page content, such as the highlighted parts in Figure 5.9.

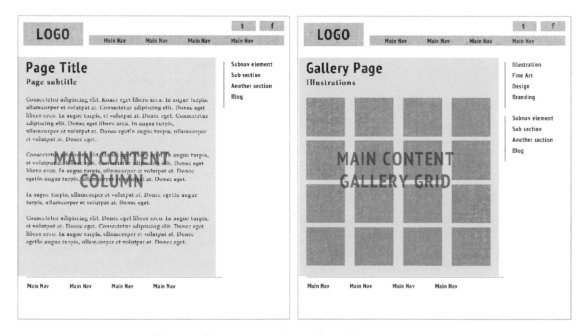

Figure 5.9. The center column is used for exclusive page content

The other column(s) will contain secondary navigation and links to related content on the site, such as the highlighted parts in Figure 5.10. Depending on the page, the main content will be configured to best suit the content.

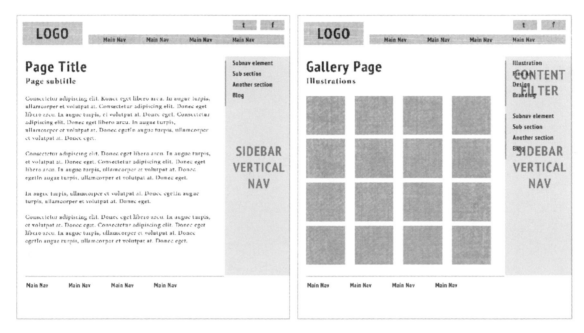

Figure 5.10. Sidebars are reserved for ancillary content, secondary navigation, and content filtering

An image gallery will probably use a grid, with each square containing a thumbnail of a larger image. If the page is for posts, you'll see a list of articles, probably with a date, title, and snippet of the full article.

Finally, below the main content area, you'll see some sort of bar at the bottom of the page. This footer to the site, indicated in Figure 5.11, will duplicate some of the functionality that the header does. It will probably provide a list of links to the main content areas, so that a user who has scrolled to the end of the page is saved from scrolling back to the top again to access a different content area.

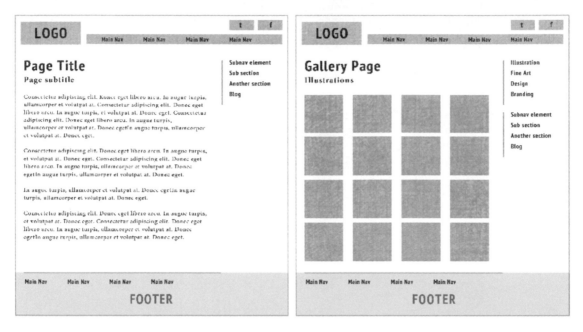

Figure 5.11. It's good practice to repeat the main navigation in the footer, particularly for long pages

The layout that I've just described is nothing more than a collection of design patterns for how a website should be laid out. These patterns work because everyone has seen them a million times. Anyone who goes to a site built with these patterns will immediately know how to reach the home page from anywhere on the site (through the main logo). They'll know that the content is organized into sections, and what each page is supposed to communicate.

Most layout patterns are common enough that we incorporate them unconsciously, but even common solutions might need editing and modification. Therefore, it's important that we know the inner workings of our own designs, instead of taking the structural elements for granted.

Architectural Patterns

Architectural patterns deal with the internal information architecture of the site and any interactions that are designed to parse that information.

Every site has an internal structure. Usually each page of the site is part of a tree structure, where the home page leads to category pages and those category pages lead to pages of a narrower focus. This common pattern for organizing the content of a site, illustrated in Figure 5.12, works well. The user is presented with a simple system for drilling down into the content to access what they want.

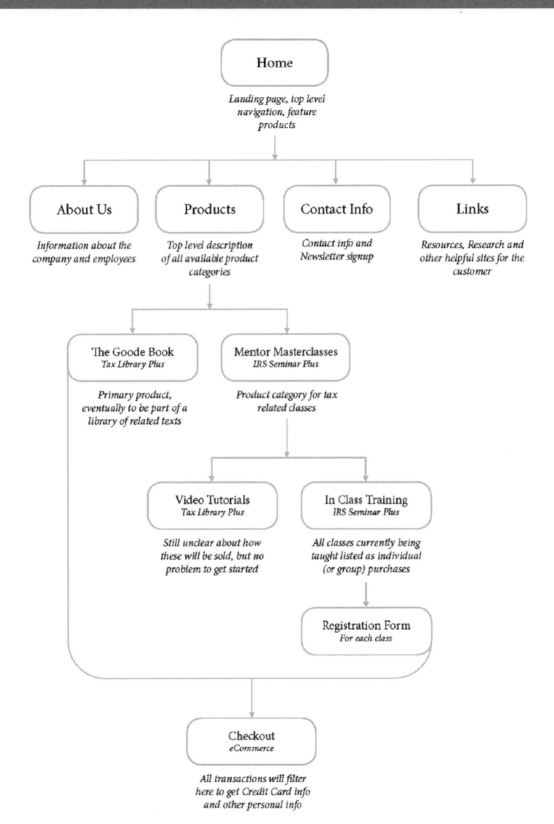

Figure 5.12. Most sites are organized into a tree structure that separates content and functionality into logical sections

Still, even with a top-down view like the one we're describing, variations in how the tree is organized can have a significant impact on the user's experience.

A site can be based on categories and subcategories, where each link in the main navigation acts as a direct connection to one of the categories, and subnavigation allows the user to focus in on each section for more detailed information. It makes sense to us because we need to compartmentalize large amounts of information. Small amounts of discrete information are easier to understand. Still, not all sites are organized in this way.

Site navigation is a major component of any successful website. Users' abilities to access the information they need is fundamental to keeping them from getting frustrated. While many sites break subnavigation into a second column or sidebar, sometimes the secondary links are embedded as text links in the actual content, giving them context and informing the user about what to expect when they click on the link.

Primary navigation links (shown at the top of Figure 5.13), by virtue of their location and prominence suggest that they link to different content areas entirely. The content found behind a primary navigation link might differ completely from the page that the user is currently viewing.

Page-specific navigation links (shown at the left of Figure 5.13), suggest that they link to content that's directly related to the current page. Their existence is contextual, so the area of the layout where page-specific links can be found will, by its very nature, be dynamic and changeable. A link found in that area should add to the content of the current page.

Contextual links are embedded directly into the content. In Figure 5.13, the sentence "We got an interview with Dr. Don Norman" makes perfect sense. The sentence tells us everything we need to know about the link. In this case, I would expect the link to take me to more information about Don Norman, or perhaps even take me to his site.

I've found that a mix of all three types of links produce enough flexibility in a design to accommodate the habits of most users.

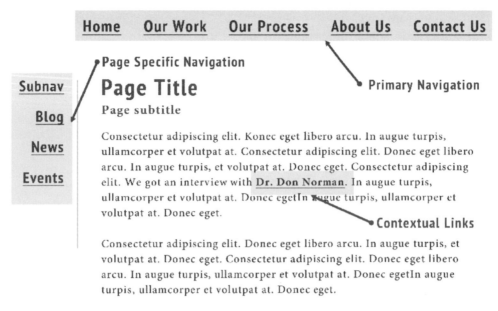

Figure 5.13. The type of link and its location can say a lot about the content that it links to

Another architectural pattern issue is how to convey a hierarchy of information when displaying content on a page. A widespread solution is borrowed from the long history of print design. Content is broken into sections with titles of varying sizes to differentiate between headings and subheadings.

This pattern of varying the sizes of text elements to communicate their relative importance is an excellent example of how a pattern is independent of its stylistic representation. Every site has a different type sensibility. Some sites have multiple fonts, while others only have one. The relative sizes of text on a site can vary greatly and the use of a font is strongly influenced by the subjective opinions of the designer.

Interaction Patterns

Patterns for interaction communicate how an onscreen element can be manipulated to achieve a particular task or to produce a desired result. This is a rapidly evolving area of patterns because of the proliferation of touchscreens among the general public. Many sites are experienced largely through touchscreen devices, and the growing familiarity with gestures and touch-based controls has led to their increased usage in desktop versions of sites. Sliders, drag-and-drop functionality, gestures, and range controls are just a few of the new interactions that are becoming more mainstream in all web applications.

Until recently, interaction on a website has been limited to filling out forms and clicking buttons. Now, even though the primary interface device is still a mouse, interface elements are becoming more directly connected to the intended purpose of the element.

For example, take a range finder, where the user selects the top and bottom numbers for whatever range they're after. In the past, this might have been handled using two form fields, as shown on the left in Figure 5.14. The user would select the first field, type in a minimum figure, then tab to the next field, and type in a maximum figure. This solution works, but requires a lot of the user.

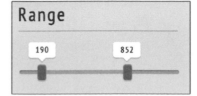

Figure 5.14. The evolution of web range finders

Here are some of the complications created by using form fields in this situation:

- Users need to know the lowest possible number that can be entered into the first field and the highest possible number that can be entered into the second field.

- They must ensure that the number entered into the first field is lower/smaller than the second.

- They have to make sure that they format their numbers properly.

- The fields don't *feel* like a range, which causes a disconnection between the two points of data and what they represent.

Hence, the problem with working with form fields here is that the action taken by users (entering a value into a field) fails to directly correlate with the task that they're attempting to complete.

A better solution would be to have a visual element that looks like a slider with two handles, as shown on the right in Figure 5.14. One handle indicates the low range value while the other is for choosing the high range value.

Conceptual Patterns

Conceptual patterns help the user build a mental model of the site and its functionality. I find this group of patterns the most difficult to explain for two reasons.

First, conceptual patterns are entirely abstract. In fact, they may be completely visible. Conceptual patterns are those that communicate the intended purpose and functionality of an interactive element. In practice, they largely inform other patterns, because conceptual patterns are primarily designed to provide the user with everything they need to create a mental model of the content.

Second, conceptual patterns are fundamentally incorporated into all patterns. We've already talked about layout patterns, which are solutions for how to arrange content on the page; header, footer, main content, and sidebar are a common configuration of page elements. It's a familiar pattern and users understand it; however, under all that structure the arrangement of page elements also implies a map for how the page content is structured.

The configuration of elements in the sidebar informs the user about what content is related to the page's main content. Groupings of elements imply an association between those included in the group. Figure 5.15 demonstrates how typographic hierarchy tells us what to read and what to ignore.

Figure 5.15. Well-structured typography helps the user to clearly organize information by importance

Similarly, interaction patterns also attempt to create a mental model, this time for actions that a user can take. Think back to the range finder that we talked about in the section called "Interaction Patterns". How well does a form with two fields communicate the action of choosing a range of numbers? Sure, the user knows that they must choose a low number and a high number to gain a result, but it's hardly intuitive.

An actual slider element with two handles provides a much clearer visual of the information that they're manipulating, including *how it's being manipulated*. They can see a complete model of the data, and are given immediate feedback about their choices; that's because the values they enter are determined by the system, so the user is restricted from entering an invalid number.

A good example of this is the Twitter Bootstrap.[5] Bootstrap is a robust HTML, CSS, and JavaScript toolkit for front-end developers. On the documentation page one line explains the difference between links and buttons: "As a convention, buttons should only be used for actions while hyperlinks are to be used for objects. For instance, 'Download' should be a button while 'recent activity' should be a link." Figure 5.16 illustrates this distinction.

Buttons do Actions!　Text links should lead to some **other content**.

Figure 5.16. The conceptual difference between buttons and links

With links and buttons, the interaction is the same: the user clicks on them with a mouse or touches them, and it does its stuff. Bootstrap is making a statement about the intent of that interaction. How can the user distinguish between a link that will move them to another area of the site and a button that will perform a certain action? Bootstrap is asserting that the visual look of a link should relate to its function. By standardizing the visual language, Bootstrap helps the user build a mental model of what certain interactions will achieve.

Bootstrap is far from being the first framework (or design) to make a visual distinction between the intended purpose of links and of buttons, but it's one of the first I've seen that explicitly states and standardizes it.

What you should take away from this is that the pattern is not how the button looks or what it accomplishes; it's the distinction between an object (a link or a button) and what it can achieve (an action).

Great, but where's the list of design patterns?

Sadly, there's no room in this book to really discuss every design pattern in existence. Instead, I took some time to introduce you to the different types of patterns and how they impact the process for structuring a site, organizing a site's content, and designing the various interactive elements.

Most of the problems you face while designing have tried-and-true solutions, and many sites have catalogued those solutions. Just knowing what the patterns are and why they exist will go a long way towards providing the tools you need to design intelligent and intuitive web pages.

Clearly, you can search for "design pattern library" online and find thousands of sites that catalog design patterns, but over time I've found a few that I prefer. This is a quick (and incomplete list):

Yahoo Design Patterns Library (http://developer.yahoo.com/ypatterns/)
> This is a nice library of patterns with fairly detailed explanations of problems the pattern solves, appropriate use cases, and pitfalls. It's not huge, but what information is there is good.

---

[5] http://twitter.github.com/bootstrap

UI Design Patterns (http://ui-patterns.com/patterns)

In this fairly strong library, the patterns are only roughly organized, but the categories view is really easy to parse. You can also join and contribute to the site.

Pattern Tap (http://patterntap.com/)

In this very large collection, many of the patterns in the library aren't strictly patterns, but they are good examples of how to utilize a combination of patterns. It's a great site to explore and see how other designers are solving problems. Of these three sites, Pattern Tap is probably my favorite, because of the great variety that it offers.

Mistaking Trends and Fashion for Design Patterns

A common misconception about design patterns is that they are examples of a style. To demonstrate, let's compare **Faceted Navigation**,[6] a design pattern for efficiently searching though content where each item has multiple categorizations, and an entry in Pattern Tap for circular images.[7] Faceted navigation and circular images have nothing in common, but I want to show you how only one is a design pattern.

Faceted navigation is a real design pattern for how to organize links that lead to categories of content. It solves a real problem that traditional navigation is unable to and gives the user a better experience when searching through certain groups of information. Faceted navigation has a real use case that is all about improving the quality of interaction for the user and nothing to do with how the navigation looks.

For instance, a user might want to find a recipe, but be unsure about what exactly they're looking for. Faceted navigation gives them multiple entry points based upon several subjects related to their search, such as "Main Ingredient," "Preparation," "Cuisine," "Season," and "Course," as shown in Figure 5.17. Instead of having to define the search criteria, the user is presented with options that can funnel them towards what they want, even if they're unclear about their final goal.

---

[6] http://www.welie.com/patterns/showPattern.php?patternID=faceted-navigation
[7] http://patterntap.com/pattern/creative-team-page-circle-images-amazee-labs

Find the Perfect Recipe

Main Ingredient

Beans, Beef, Berries, Cheese, Chocolate, Citrus, Dairy, Eggs, Fish, Fruits, Garlic, Ginger, Grains, Greens, Herbs, Lamb, Mushrooms, Mustard, Nuts, Nuts, Olives, Onions, Pasta, Peppers, Pork, Potatoes, Poultry, Rice, Shellfish, Tomatoes, Vegetables

Cuisine

African, American, Caribbean, Eastern, European, French, Greek, Italian, Jewish, Mediterranean, Mexican, Middle Eastern, Scandinavian, Spanish

Preparation

Advanced, Bake, Broil, Fry, Grill, Marinade, Microwave, No Cook, Poach, Quick, Roast, Saute, Slow Cook, Steam, Stir Fry

Season

Christmas, Easter, Fall, Fourth of July, Hanukkah, New Years, Picnics, Spring, Summer, Super Bowl, Thanksgiving, Valentine's Day, Winter

Course

Appetizers, Bread, Breakfast, Deserts, Main Course, Salads, Sandwiches, Sauces, Side Dish, Snacks

Figure 5.17. The faceted navigation pattern is good for occasions when the user might approach a subject from multiple avenues

The Pattern Tap example shown in Figure 5.18, however, is not a design pattern in the strictest sense. The treatment of each image on the page is interesting and fairly unique, but the fact that each image is contained in a circle instead of a rectangle is really just a presentation treatment. I would accept that the design uses the gallery pattern for presenting a group of small article-like content elements, but the visual treatment is another matter altogether.

Figure 5.18. While the circular images are an awesome visual effect, they are not a design pattern

Rounded corners, inset text, and ribbons?

In the end, all I really want is for you to know that design patterns exist, understand how to evaluate them in the wild, and incorporate them into your workflow. Inevitably, you will come across problems where most patterns are unsatisfactory for your needs; however, most of the time they can help you make quick decisions when faced with a design challenge that you're struggling to understand.

In the next chapter, we'll talk about two subjects: conceptual design, and the process for creating a final mockup. Prepare for the fireworks!

Chapter 6

Conceptual Design and Our Color Project

This is the point where you're probably pulling your hair out and trying to decide if it's possible to throttle me through the book. I mean, really! This is supposed to be a design book and we're yet to design anything!

I feel your pain. I, too, succumb to that little voice (given a face in Figure 6.1) that says, "Why are you wasting time with this stuff? Just crack open Photoshop. Trust your gut. Mood boards are for sissies."

Figure 6.1. Ignore the little voice insisting that you cut corners

But you have to be strong. That voice is just plain wrong.

The truth is that we've been designing the entire time we've been moving through the book. We've addressed the major facets of a designer's job in the previous chapters except for the creation of the final mockup, and let me tell you: the final mockup is the easy part if you've done your homework.

By taking the time to go through all the phases of our process, presented in Figure 6.2, we give ourselves the tools and the information needed to truly understand what it is we're designing. We know the problems that we are solving for our client because we know the client and we've dug into the content. We know what our art direction will be because we understand the content and we've chosen appropriate imagery and visuals. We can design the site's internal architecture and page layout because we know what is important and how best to present it.

Figure 6.2. A website is built on many layers of process, of which the mockup is a small part

How can we possibly create a great design if we lack those tools? Sure, we could crack open Photoshop (just like that evil voice suggests) and we might make a pretty mockup, but design is about more than making things pretty. It's about making things beautiful, functional, and cohesive. It's about solving a problem and thinking about every aspect of the product and the design.

Where do we go from here?

When creating a design, or a series of related designs, I often find it helpful to find the items, ideas, and visuals that will be used. We've undergone quite a bit of process to attain the visual and structural elements that we need for our design. Now it's time to think about the conceptual elements that tie everything together.

Conceptual Design: Just a Little Black Magic

When I talk about **conceptual design**, I'm referring to an idea that guides the design. I'm not talking about the parts of the design that help build mental models, or the parts of a design that exemplify the brand. Nor is this about the visuals of the design.

Instead, I'm referring to a theme or idea that's fundamental to all the design decisions that are made. This is a fairly difficult idea to explain in words, so I'll use some concepts that I've developed over the last few years for our Converge SE conference.[1]

Idea-driven Design

"Usually, when I get the project request, I will send out a questionnaire to get a feel for what the project is about … Once we go through that initial process of getting the client's input on what they think they want … I will set up a kick-off call where I ask a lot of questions. When I first started out, it was mainly focused on [topics] like, 'what colors should the site be and what kind of imagery do you want?' because, as a designer, that's all I really cared about. But now, I try to get a sense of who the user is and what their motivation is for coming to the site or using the product. [I want] a feel for the personality of the brand more than just what colors to use."

—Meagan Fisher

Converge SE is a two-day web conference. The first day is usually five streams of workshops to choose from and the second day consists of keynote presentations. The format is fairly typical of web conferences, but we've managed to create an interesting brand with our site designs and through the tone that we like to set, as conveyed in Figure 6.3.

Figure 6.3. With conceptual design, the look and feel of a site is guided by the concept

In many ways, the process by which I reach a design is fairly linear. First, I start by asking myself questions. In the case of Converge SE, the questions I've asked over the last three years have been:

---

[1] http://convergese.com/

- What is a conference?
- Why do people attend conferences?
- What is Converge SE's mission?
- Why do some people become speakers and not others?
- What do attendees really take away from a conference?
- Do people attend for information or for some other purpose?

I ask these questions because they get to the heart of the content for the conference site. By doing this, I can find a central idea to draw from.

According to Gene, the main organizer of Converge SE, the conference had been created with a particular mission in mind. Gene wanted an event where designers, developers, and businesspeople could experience and learn about what they all do. Designers could attend some of the development streams and learn more about back-end work. Developers could learn about the business side of web industry. Business people could learn about the creative and technical hurdles that their employees jump through every day. This philosophy is expressed in Figure 6.4.

Figure 6.4. Converge is about the connections that can form between people with completely different skill sets

Converge SE really means: a convergence of all the parts of the web industry. I really liked the idea, so, in 2009, I latched onto the notion that Converge SE is really an intersection of multiple worlds. It's a collision of disciplines and a blending of different kinds of people.

This became the central concept for the design. But, that still begs the question, "How do I turn this idea into visuals?"

Creative Association

I find that the best way to translate an idea into visuals is to brainstorm it, the same way that you would with design decisions. For Converge, I wanted enticing and provocative visuals to stir up conversation, yet I was after a theme that could support multiple illustrations, intuitively demonstrating the meaning of "Converge."

First, I thought about other words that relate to Converge, synonyms that produced strong visuals in my mind. "Smash," "collide," "unite," "unify," and "assemble" were some of the words I came up with. I wanted words that conveyed some kind of action. Think about it. When you read the word "smash," it produces a form of visual in your mind, such as in Figure 6.5, right?

Figure 6.5. Words like "smash" can be highly visual; they can be seen and felt

> "The play time that's involved on every project, or every problem-solving exercise, is the most important part for me. So, if there's anything that I try to always do, [it's to] have enough time to … think, play, and explore …"
>
> —Dan Rubin

So, I mulled the words over in my mind, allowing any visual ideas to just pop up when I thought about them in relation to Converge. "Collide" and "smash" made me think of *War of the Worlds*, which would have been great fodder for art and humor, but failed to really match Converge's mission. Converge is supposed to be about collaboration and understanding, rather than conflict.

"Unite" and "assemble" made me think of the possibilities that could come from combining different items to produce a concept that was new and better. I thought about combining robotics and humans, but it felt a little dystopian when I started sketching. I thought about some sort of magical reality, where fantasy is mixed with the real world. In short, I started thinking of ideas that would be visually rich, and would provide a narrative that expressed the conference's core mission.

> "When I start a new project and I'm first exploring an idea, I'll try to limit the scope of what I'm setting out to do …"
>
> —Shaun Inman

After a bit of sketching and deliberating, I settled on an idea that I called "Strange Menagerie." The central idea of this was that the conference website would be a glimpse into a land where every animal in the Converge world is a combination of two animals. The world had to be realistic because I wanted the strangeness of the smashed-together elements to be starkly contrasted against a world that seemed remarkably familiar.

This is where you're thinking, "That's weird, Gio. You are a strange fellow."

Yes, indeed, it's weird … but consider that the strangeness of this idea is part of its appeal for these reasons:

- It makes perfect sense, in a visceral way. The art and the name have an intuitive connection that many people understood right away.

- The art is entertaining and evocative. Seriously, three years later people still talk to me about the deerstrich and the rabbass, the latter which is seen in Figure 6.6.

Figure 6.6. The "rabbass" from the Converge SE 2010 Strange Menagerie

- The artwork got people talking about the site, and therefore talking about the conference. The exposure that we gained by being a little left-field was invaluable.

- It gave us a definitive brand. Converge is now well known for the kind of sites we produce. Attendees have insight into the way that we think, and they feel better connected to us. Rather than being about weird animals, our brand is about creativity, risk-taking, and individuality.

Art Direction

The point of all this conceptual exploration is that the central idea has a lot of influence on design choices. Tone, copy, art, and style can all be influenced by a concept, and can be much more cohesive for it.

I've also found that by designing towards a concept, I let the concept guide my decisions, so I end up developing more interesting and unique visuals. The concept drives me down paths that I might otherwise never have taken.

Illustration and Art

The artwork was worked up in two levels. Detailed pencil sketches, such as the sharktopus in Figure 6.7, were used on the splash page site, social media sites, and most of the documentation and print materials.

Figure 6.7. The Converge SE mascot: love him, fear him

Every major section of the site featured a painting of a different animal. We decided that full-color art would have more impact on the site than pencil drawings, as shown in Figure 6.8.

Figure 6.8. Every major page featured a new creature from the Strange Menagerie

In addition to the animal drawings and paintings, I also worked with a 3D artist to produce a short CGI movie of one of the animals. The video was shown during the conference and on the site. Figure 6.9 shows a screenshot from it. I have to admit, this was one of my favorite art assets. It was definitely a labor of love and I couldn't have done it without Bryce Bigger of Bigger Design.

Figure 6.9. We even made a 3D animated video of our main mascot

Finally, I produced line drawings of each of the speakers as different animals, seen in Figure 6.10. Kevin Hale was a scorpion (I think). Matthew Smith was a whale. Fun stuff. The speaker illustrations were used in some of the print materials, but didn't make it onto the site. They were a way of *integrating all the parts of the conference with the concept.* The speakers' faces were familiar, the attendees had come to hear them speak, but they were changed to fit with our art and design.

Figure 6.10. Some of the speakers as their animal selves

Design Elements and Style

The design was heavily influenced by the idea that the Strange Menagerie is an alien world. The colors were earthy blues and browns overlaid with natural textures and soft gradients. While highly structured, the design is clearly asymmetrical and freely mixes art and content, as Figure 6.11 shows.

Figure 6.11. Each design element was influenced by the theme and concept to create a harmonious and continuous style

The logo was a hand-drawn version of a nice, fat serif typeface. We really liked the way the typeface read, but it lacked the right tone for the site. It felt a little bookish, and we wanted it to feel more natural and closer to a well-done scribble than a vector font. It also provided a good contrast with the live text on the site and tied together the vector art with the hand-drawn images.

Dividing lines and boxes were hand-drawn and scanned in. The typefaces chosen were clear and easy to read, though ever-so-slightly grungy in their visual appeal, as Figure 6.12 shows.

CONVERGE SE
JU 26710 *~

Figure 6.12. Lines, textures, and design elements were hand-drawn and scanned in to match the hand-drawn feel of the artwork

By taking cues from the concept, the design became well integrated with all the art assets. It gave the art and content structure and context, so that users could find what they were looking for, instead of being distracted by the visuals. In short, the design became part of the content.

Practical Implementation of an Idea

Never discount the power of a central unifying idea. The emotional impact of a thought-provoking design can be rewarding for both designer and user. If you choose to develop a creative concept, let it guide your decisions. I find that designing is easier if I'm clear about what I'm designing, why I'm designing it, and how the design will be used to communicate the content, as Figure 6.13 shows.

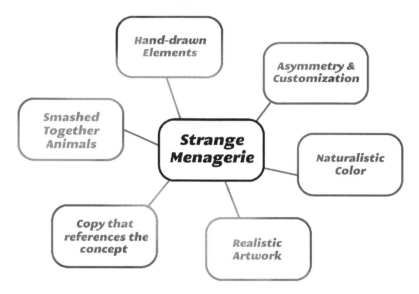

Figure 6.13. The concept—the central idea—guides everything from structure to tone and style

For an idea to work, such as the one created for Converge, it needs to function on multiple layers:

- The work has to be good. Following a concept is no excuse for bad design.

- The visuals must be engaging and set the right tone. If the user is unable to understand the concept, they should be able to view the design and enjoy its formal qualities, regardless of any deeper meaning.

- The narrative that the design establishes should relate directly to the content. You want to avoid creating a design that's utterly confusing. Creating a design that piques the user's curiosity and requires a little exploration is fine, but if users are constantly asking themselves what's going on, your concept is probably inappropriate or convoluted.

When Not to Be Clever

Sometimes a budget fails to justify the additional time expense of conceptual design, or the client has solid ideas about what they want. Perhaps the content has no need for any unifying concept or the company brand already has a strong conceptual direction. Sometimes you'll just lack good ideas related to a particular project. Whatever the reason, sometimes it just doesn't work out.

On those occasions, follow the other steps of the process and produce a great design. Like I said before, conceptual design isn't a requirement of web design. No one is expecting it, but I've found that having a conceptual basis produces better designs.

This brings us to Spectrumagic.

Spectrumagic

Figure 6.14 shows our Spectrumagic logo.

Figure 6.14. The Spectrumagic logo

"I've been using Photoshop long enough that I can move fairly quickly, but it's also a hindrance because [I'm] tempted to start really styling things right away instead of focusing on the higher level interactions … 'Am I showing the right data?' as opposed to 'Am I showing the data correctly?' So, I'm cautious about going straight into Photoshop, and I try not to get sidetracked by matters of style for as long as possible."

—Daniel Burka

So, we've taken the long road towards a design. We've covered quite a bit of material, and now we need to see the fruits of our labor so that we can create our final mockups. Over the next few sections, we'll take a look at all the assets that have been created for the Spectrumagic project. We'll review their purpose and discuss the ways that they inform our final designs. Finally, we'll go through the process of designing the mockups. By the end of this chapter, we'll have complete designs that can be sent off for client approval.

Yeah!

Content

In this case, we've been provided with the content we need for the site, which isn't always the case. Clients frequently fail to provide content of any kind early on in a project. Avoid being fooled into designing without content if you can avoid it.

> "The more time I spend up front [in discovery], the better the project goes. I try to spend at least a week really digging into user research and getting a sense of the content goals for the site. Before doing a wireframe or anything design-oriented, we'll talk about the main call to action [and] the key content for each page, and try to outline that first."
>
> —Meagan Fisher

You have to ask yourself "If the site is information-based, what am I really designing?"

The answer is that you're designing information (and interaction). If you lack the information, how can you design it? Seems straightforward to me.

If the client is slow in giving you the required content to work from, then at least gain a sense of what the content will be. Think of it like journalism. Journalists try to find out the "who, what, when, where, why, and how" of a story, which is just another way of saying that they try to gain all the pertinent details. You should try to do the same. Make the client explain all the content goals. Ask them to explain what information will go where.

Remember way back in the section called "Ask Questions" in Chapter 3, we drafted our "Need to Know" list. That list was designed to act as a bridge between you and the client. You need to know what you're up for with a project. That initial client interview is key to learning the "who, what, when, where, why, and how" of a design project.

> "I think it's a cop-out when designers say they get handed bad copy. If I'm working [on] a bed-and-breakfast website, and the owner of the bed-and-breakfast gives me a 20,000-word essay on why the deluxe room is a great room, as a designer it's not my role to just do my best with it. My role is to say, 'that's not going to make a good product.' [I] try to explain to the client [that] a potential customer is going to visit the page, [so] what is it we are trying to achieve here? This is basic product direction stuff."
>
> —Daniel Burka

You'll also recall that the client provided some basic project parameters. Some of those parameters defined the brand goals and use cases, but others described content goals. Let's isolate those parameters and make sure that we have our content straight.

- Spectrumagic is an educational site about color. It is a highly interactive and dynamic experience that teaches the reader about the science of visible color and the practical application of color theory.

- It is primarily designed for high-school students, but should be accessible to middle-school students and adults as well.

■ It will include extensive content that is broken into two distinct categories: the science of color, and color theory. Each category will have a quiz that users can take to test their knowledge about the category. Half the quiz will comprise multiple-choice questions, while the other half will be an interactive game.

Spectrumagic's project parameters give us a good sense of the content goals, but not the details of the discrete pieces of content or content hierarchy. To clearly understand content flow, I like to produce outlines that are structured the way the site will be.

Spectrumagic is a small site. It only has about ten pages, but we want to build it to be flexible.

The outline can then be used to produce a sitemap, seen in Figure 6.15.

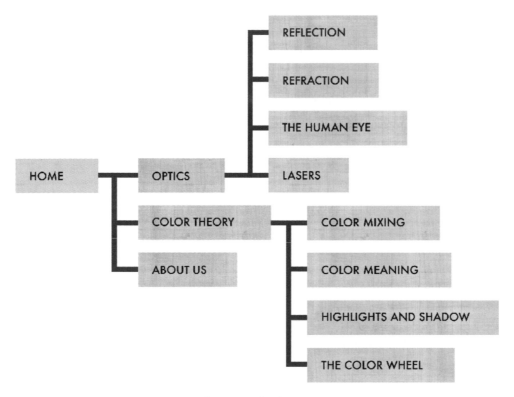

Figure 6.15. Our sitemap

A description of the content goals, a hierarchical outline of the content, and a sitemap should be enough to make you laser-focused on content. By digging through each part of the content and helping to shape it, you'll have a much better understanding of what you're designing for. Often the sites we design are about subjects we know nothing of. Have you ever heard of fly ash? Neither had I until I helped build a website for a fly ash refinery. Now I know it's a byproduct of combustion that's refined and used as an aggregate in construction materials. Who knew?

Now that we have a handle on our content, let's take a look at the wireframes we produced for Spectrumagic.

Wireframes

I took a really simple strategy with the Spectrumagic wireframes, seen in Figure 6.16.

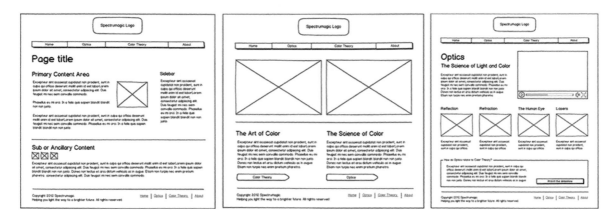

Figure 6.16. Spectrumagic wireframes

I wanted them to be a fair mix of general layout and content focus. Remember that these designs need to be responsive, so I'm using the wireframes to develop my page content hierarchy as well. I find it difficult to create multiple wireframes for each breakpoint in a responsive design. Instead, I only create wireframes for the desktop version of a site. Because I know that the HTML will be the same for all devices, I can safely design for a large form factor, all the while keeping in mind that the order of elements matters.

With Spectrumagic, I tried to ensure that all the columns and content blocks flow logically when at smaller sizes. Because mobile devices often stack content vertically, you want to make sure that the markup is ordered hierarchically, with content cascading down the page in order of importance. This will also support SEO and accessibility.

Additionally, consider elements that will appear after larger breakpoints, but not at mobile sizes. Many home pages have a large **hero unit**, where the main tagline for the site and a large image or slider appears, such as the highlighted part of Figure 6.17. At mobile sizes, elements like that lose their luster; they look scrunched and out of place. Luckily, hero units often contain only a couple of important elements surrounded by a lot of fluff. The only real content is the tagline, so the image can disappear when the site becomes too small, leaving a line of text that functions more like a page title. Alternatively, a portion of the image could be shown.

Figure 6.17. The featured area (in red) has decorative elements that can disappear at mobile sizes without adversely affecting usability

Elements that appear in multiple locations can also be judiciously hidden. Depending on how the elements stack vertically, only the first instance of the link might need to be visible, as Figure 6.18 shows.

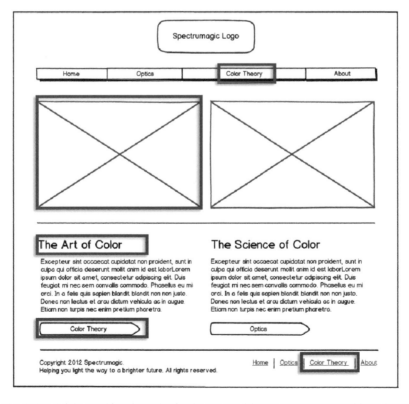

Figure 6.18. As a responsive design shrinks, consider what redundancies you can delete to conserve space without detracting from functionality

Laying out Mobile Designs

Usually, I refrain from putting together wireframes for mobile-sized layouts, unless they're quite complex. Instead, I work up mobile-sized designs after I've written the HTML. I find it easier to design the desktop version of the site so that I have content hierarchy worked out, and then to use the natural flow of the HTML to determine how the mobile version of the site should stack. We'll certainly need to consider the way that the site will be marked up because the HTML will determine how items flow and in what order they'll appear.

In this case, I'll show you some wireframes of how I might shift around the content for different screen sizes. We'll use the home page wireframe to dig into this.

Let's break down the process of translating a wide site to a small site.

1. Start with the desktop wireframe

The point to keep in mind with our desktop website wireframe is that, in the simplest terms, all websites are basically text documents that have been formatted with CSS. The structural wireframe that you see is really a list of items that are stacked vertically and nested hierarchically. To line up elements horizontally, we float them left or right with the CSS `float` property, as in Figure 6.19.

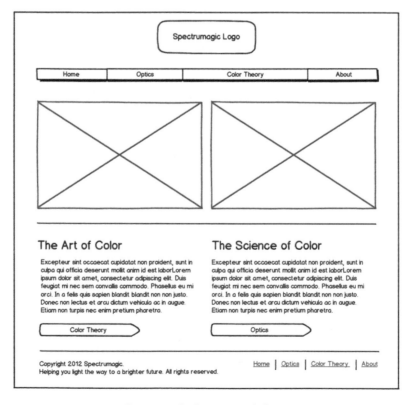

Figure 6.19. Our home page wireframe

2. Identify the main site areas

HTML is a semantic outline of the page content. Without CSS, the page elements will stack vertically. In our wireframe in Figure 6.20, these areas naturally stack this way. These areas will be completely fluid, which means that they'll expand and contract with the browser, regardless of the content inside them.

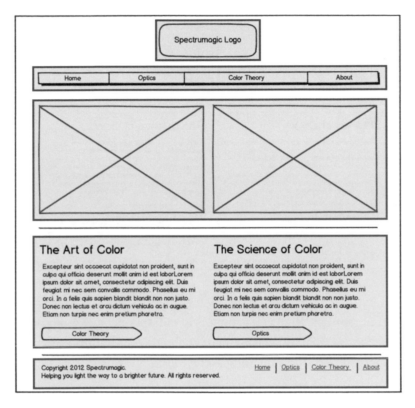

Figure 6.20. The completely fluid elements in our design

The fluid behavior of these areas is an asset when trying to make a design responsive, because the only items that really need to change are items they contain.

3. Identify the areas that will be affected by breakpoints

Every responsive design has breakpoints, where the layout changes in response to media queries for different browser sizes. At wider browser sizes, areas are floated or horizontally aligned with floats in our design; this works perfectly fine and the design can be 100% fluid, but the layout will start to break down at mobile sizes. Text blocks, like "The Art of Color" and "The Science of Color" seen in Figure 6.21, will be so narrow that the columns of text will look strange and long words will break out of their containers. The main nav bar will start to look strange because the last link will likely break to the next line.

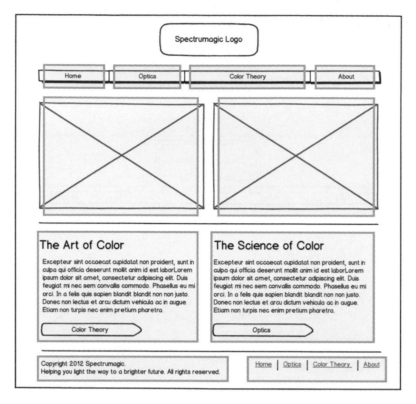

Figure 6.21. Elements that will respond to breakpoints

Having a design that reorganizes the page elements at smaller sizes can rectify all these problems. At mobile sizes, many of the floated page elements—the ones lined up horizontally—will stack vertically. Other elements are redundant and can be rendered invisible at smaller sizes.

 Show the Good Stuff

Some designers prefer to avoid hiding elements at mobile sizes, even if they are redundant. In essence, I agree, but sometimes it makes sense. If you have five links to the same page on your home page, it's likely some will be unnecessary at mobile sizes, where screen real estate is that much more precious. Never hide real content from your users, but for redundant elements, use your own judgment.

4. Decide how the breakpoints will affect each area

We'll address each of the four major areas that will respond to breakpoints in turn. In this design, determining the breakpoints is fairly simple. I think that one breakpoint will suffice. We have no sidebar to consider and the design never has more than two equal columns. In most cases, we'll just stack our elements vertically instead of horizontally. The following refers to Figure 6.22.

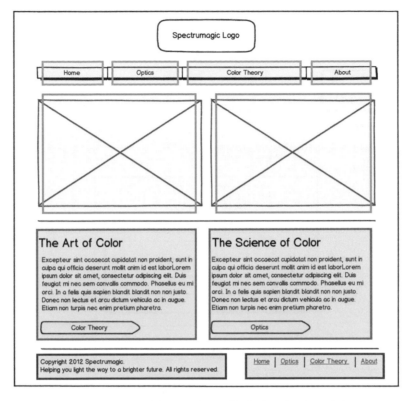

Figure 6.22. Each of the areas that we'll talk about is color coded

The navigation bar (in green) is quite straightforward. The navigation will likely be an unordered list with each element floated to the left. All we need to do is disable the floats at smaller browser sizes; that way the navigation items will stack vertically.

The hero unit (in orange) will work a little differently. Our hero unit contains two images that link to content areas. The links in these images are repeated in the content areas (shown in purple) and the images add little except eye candy. In this case, we'll just ax the entire hero unit and let the content start higher in the document.

The content areas and the footer elements (in blue) are easy enough as well. We'll simply stack them vertically, the same as we did with the navigation to achieve our final mobile-sized design.

You can see that each element is still available for the mobile site and many of the components don't even need to be changed. Instead, they get shifted and restacked. The navigation is transformed into a vertical list of buttons, all the better for big fingers, as shown in Figure 6.23. Redundancies in the content are removed, streamlining the page for reduced scrolling. All content is given the full width of the mobile device for easy reading, as seen in Figure 6.24.

Desktop

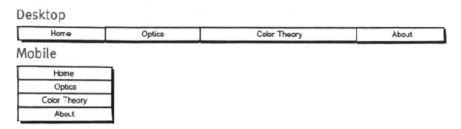

Mobile

Figure 6.23. Restacking the navigation: horizontal at large sizes, vertical at small sizes

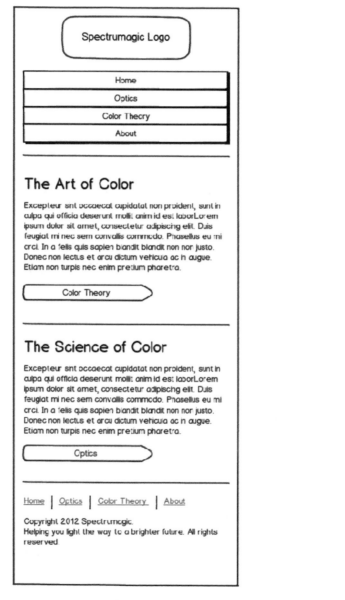

Figure 6.24. The final mobile wireframe

What we've just done is to utilize some common mobile design patterns to make our site work across all devices. The code necessary to achieve these results is beyond the scope of this book, but if you want to dig into media queries and learn how to use `min-width`-determined breakpoints to great effect, check out Jay Barry's article on Unmatched Style.[2] Jay goes into great detail about the benefits of marking up responsive sites practically.

How do we make all these wireframes?

So, we have a number of wireframes at our disposal. In this case, I've used Balsamiq to mock up the Spectrumagic wireframes. I prefer dedicated wireframing tools because they offer additional functionality, unlike programs such as Illustrator. For instance, Balsamiq lets me treat any element like a link. So, if I add an "About Us" button to the home page wireframe, I can link that button to the "About Us" wireframe. Once I have all my wireframes, I can link them together and click through links just like a real website. It's a great way to rapidly prototype a website or app, and you can use your Balsamiq projects to demonstrate functionality to the client.

However, having a dedicated app for wireframing isn't a requirement. Lately, I've even heard of designers using Keynote to draft their wireframes. It matters little which tool you use to complete the job.

> "I usually sketch wireframes out with pen and paper first, and from there I'll go into markup. I like making wireframes in markup. It forces me to focus on the content because [I'm] building out semantic, standards-based HTML first, and I think that's where every project should start."
>
> —Meagan Fisher

Our project is an interesting case. Spectrumagic has two main fields of content (Optics and Color Theory) that are related, but distinct. I tried to put together wireframes that have a definite structure, but also allow movement between the two content areas when one piece of information is relevant to another. For instance, on the Optics page, near the bottom, is a box that links to content in the Color Theory page. The design should emphasize where the content areas overlap and how they relate to one another.

The home page wireframe, shown in Figure 6.19, is fairly simple. Its main function is to funnel users into either of the two content areas. Both areas are given equal emphasis, because the site is primarily interested in informing the user, rather than forcing them down a particular path. In addition, because the content is interlinked in subpages, it's of no consequence which path they choose, as the user will inevitably see a little of both content areas.

The content-area wireframes (Optics and Color Theory) act as content overviews, and are shown in Figure 6.25. They give a general description of the content in their area, provide a video or mul-

---

[2] http://unmatchedstyle.com/news/working-with-media-queries-and-min-width.php

timedia experience to introduce the area, and emphasize the primary subjects covered by their content areas.

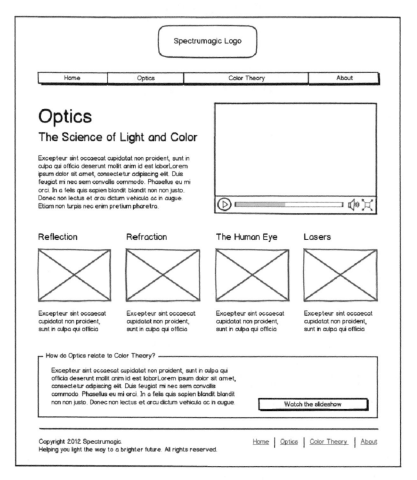

Figure 6.25. The wireframe for our two main content areas

I've laid out this page for maximum flexibility. Subpage content can be added by simply adding another element to the gallery below the page content. The wireframe shows four elements, but because the gallery is a regular grid, new elements can be added easily.

The subpage wireframe was more difficult to design, as each of these pages could be heavily customized. The Color Wheel, as pictured in Figure 6.26, is just an example page. A large image of the color wheel is appropriate on this page, but the Color Mixing page might have some sort of game instead, or an interactive demonstration of color mixing. Other pages might have no large image or interactive element at the beginning.

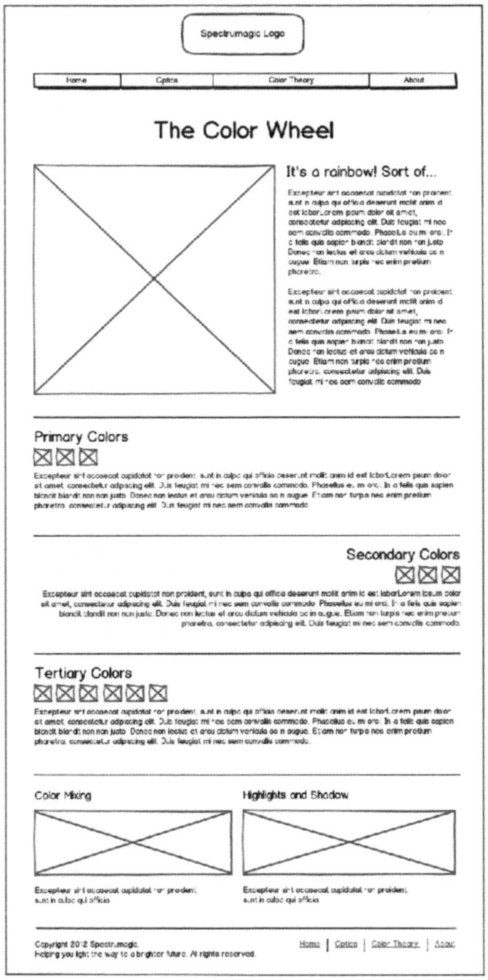

Figure 6.26. Each of the deep content pages are heavily customized for the content

Figure 6.27 shows three main areas. The top area is dedicated to the main content and interactive elements for the page. The second area is dedicated to related information in the form of text and images. The third area is used to link to related materials, other content pages, and external sources.

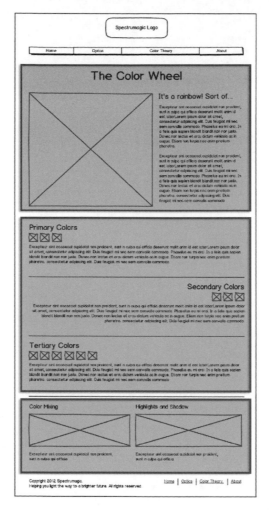

Figure 6.27. The three main areas that will need to appear on each content subpage

Each wireframe is kept simple. The interactive elements (games and such) will have to be designed and integrated on a per-page basis anyway, so I'm treating these wireframes as structural documents; they are focused on how the user moves around the site and how the content will be consistently displayed.

Art Direction

"If anything, experience [working on design projects] has taught me more about the way that works well for me, and I change it up depending on who I'm working with. When I'm working with … a team, I tend to have more of a process because [it] combines various creative approaches. So, everyone has their own way of doing things, but you can unify everyone with common milestones … to guide people through that winding path [of design]."

—Dan Rubin

Art direction can cover a lot of topics, but we're going to be very straightforward about it. Some art directors are in charge of production schedules and final approvals, or they might make the initial decisions about a project and sign off on any production work that comes from the designers. Other art directors take a much more hands-on approach, and create a lot of the production art that goes into the final designs.

For our Spectrumagic project, we're acting as creative director, art director, and lead designer, so it pays to distinguish the parts that each role plays. In general, creative direction involves developing a central concept, brand integration, message development, and tone. I think of the creative director as the person who articulates how the goals of a project are tied to its execution.

Once the creative director has chosen a solid direction, crystallized the message, and chosen how the project will be included in the brand, the art director can start making concrete decisions about how the project will look and function. This is where the rubber hits the road. Art direction is about producing the designs and elements that address a client's needs. We've created a number of assets that are designed to address different parts of the issue. You already know what these elements are, so let's go through the ones that we created for Spectrumagic and see what insights they provide.

Our Concept

Spectrumagic has a very strong brand aesthetic which I'd prefer to avoid disturbing. With the site, I tried to think of a means of conveying the two content areas in a unified way. At first, I kicked around the idea of having two design styles applied to the same structural wireframes and differentiating the content areas visually, but the result created too much visual noise and dissonance.

Spectrumagic is a good example of a site that doesn't need a conceptual design because the content and brand are more than enough to carry a user's interest. Instead of dedicating time and energy towards crafting a concept, I decided to work up some of the artwork that the site will use.

I wanted the art to resemble a mix of scientific illustrations and crafty art drawings, as seen in Figure 6.28. The effect is that it combines the two content areas instead of differentiating between them. I found this to be nice art direction, and a compromise between concept and content.

Figure 6.28. Spectrumagic's artwork is a mix of painterly and technical

I showed you my work on Converge so that you could see how I approach a site that does employ a concept in the process. Spectrumagic, while cool, has no need for that level of complexity.

Reference Material

We collected quite a bit of reference material early on in this project. Old designs that we want to reference and the client's list of project parameters both qualify as reference materials. So does anything else that we might want to incorporate into the design or content, such as Figure 6.29.

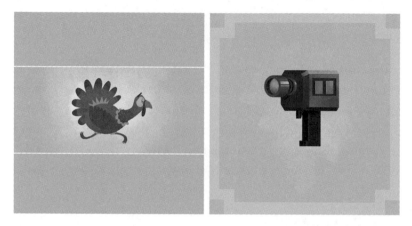

Figure 6.29. Reference materials play an important role in setting the look and tone for a design

We have a number of works that we're using as inspiration for the final design. Because of the subject's content, we want to keep the design fairly clean and simple without becoming boring. I have some relevant posters that show a solid aesthetic, and also gathered some type and illustration samples, a website featuring the structure I'm looking for, some old drawings from a 1950s children's science book, and a couple of sets of color swatches.

In addition to the visual assets that I've gathered, I must remember the branded Spectrumagic logo and its color palette. The most fundamental piece of art aside from the content will be the logo. It has a strong visual style and color palette that is impossible to ignore. You may recall when we made our mood boards, we started with that element.

Mood Boards

The mood boards that we created are designed to integrate the Spectrumagic brand with the site's content. They showcase possible typefaces, textures, colors, and design elements that we might use in the final design. The mood board is really a communication piece, used to convey our thoughts about how the design could look to the client.

Remember, a mood board is not a design. It's unlikely you'll lift whole sections of it for the final mockup. It's a source of inspiration that helps you down a particular visual path.

Even though a mood board serves an abstract purpose, in no way should you discount its power to help you solidify your visual ideas. It's a tool. In this case, we've drawn on some of the reference materials that we gathered, as well as some of the more formal design elements that could be used.

Style Tiles

Samantha Warren introduced the idea of Style Tiles[3] for use as design tools in 2011 and they've been gaining traction. The idea behind Style Tiles is that it's impractical to create custom designs for every page of a website, so instead of focusing on designing pages, we should focus on producing a *design system*. Figure 6.30 shows the default Style Tile template that Samantha supplies on her site. It's quite clear about what goes where and why.

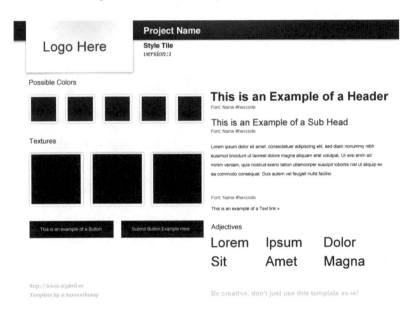

Figure 6.30. The default Style Tile template

A Style Tile is halfway between a mood board and a mockup, and is highly structured. The Style Tile at the top of Figure 6.31 shows how headers, logos, and repeating patterns will look. On the left, there are text links, buttons, and a hierarchy of typographic treatments ranging form large headers to small body copy. On the right, the color palettes and image treatments are presented as regular grids. Finally, on the bottom right, different elements are arranged a little more organically to demonstrate the variety that will be present in the design.

---

[3] http://styletil.es/

Figure 6.31. All the pieces to the web design puzzle

So, in a way, a Style Tile is a design, just not a website design. It's a system. You design the Style Tile, then go back and forth with the client over the details until everyone's satisfied. Then you move on to thumbnails, layouts, and mockups. The benefit is that when the time comes to create the final mockup, most of the decisions about design elements have already been made.

I'm fairly new to the Style Tile process; we've only used it on a few client projects, but I can already see the potential. On the website, Samantha suggests that Style Tiles are appropriate when a mood board lacks the distinctiveness, but a complete mockup is overkill.

Style Tiles were created out of a need for a more structured approach than a mood board, but without dedicating the time to a full-blown mockup. It also solves the problem of designing for websites that are constantly expanding, because you're designing a system as opposed to a single page. If you rely on mockups alone, each new page is a whole new design. If instead you rely on a system of design features and interactive elements, new pages are easier to design because they are a new configuration of the same elements.

Style Tiles also aid in any team design process because they act as guidelines for decisions that are made. When a designer deviates from the Style Tile, it's obvious. The Style Tile is both a visual framework for the website and a document of design assets, because any element in the Style Tile PSD can be copied and pasted into a mockup. Consistency is guaranteed, and if new elements are needed they can be added.

I've created a Style Tile for Spectrumagic in Figure 6.32. We'll pretend that we went through a number of iterations until the client was happy with all the design choices made.

Figure 6.32. The Spectrumagic Style Tile includes all the elements and design treatments to be used in the final design

Our Style Tile is designed to present a number of elements that might show up in our final mockup, and demonstrate how they'll appear. It can be used to direct a conversation with the client and show them how you want the design to look.

Remember, a Style Tile is system design. By having a document that shows how individual elements will display, what colors and textures to use, and how the typography should be formatted, you'll have a document that any designer can reference when working on the site.

Thumbnails and Detail Sketches

I'm going to bypass pasting in all the little sketches that I did for our Spectrumagic design. Suffice to say that I like to sketch, so there are many. Instead, I'll just show you the ones that influenced the final design in Figure 6.33. Because of my art background, I have a tendency to focus on imagery and the message behind the content. I find that thumbnails help me to focus my attention on the layout, because I'm prevented from being caught up in the little details, like I am when I'm working in Photoshop.

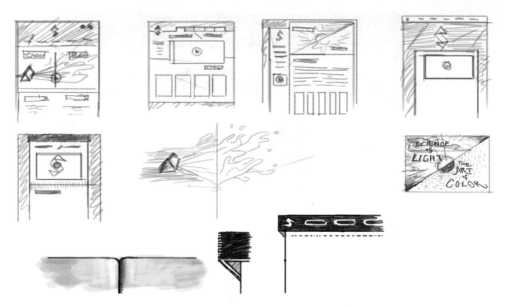

Figure 6.33. Thumbnails allow us to try out different ideas and then pick and choose the best parts

"When I start a new project and I'm first exploring an idea, I'll try to limit the scope of what I'm setting out to do …"

—Shaun Inman

I also enjoy iterating with thumbnails because the process is so fast. Once I have a number of ideas, there's the luxury of picking and choosing the best elements from all the designs and compositing them together into a final mockup.

You'll notice that some elements were used in the final designs as art, while others were altered to better suit the content; a lot of the first thumbnail and the fourth (along the top) got in. I like this mix-and-match approach, as I escape feeling hemmed in.

The Final Mockups

Final design time! Woot! We've come a long way, so I'll skip the philosophy. Let's get to it.

The Home Page

The home page in Figure 6.34 is a straight conversion from the wireframe. We have a header with navigation and branding. Underneath, we have a main hero unit with two calls to action. Finally, below that is a main content area with two blocks of content. In reality, the home page is a document with four links that take you to one of two major content areas.

Figure 6.34. The wireframe was designed first because much of the legwork had been done with the Style Tile

I did diverge from the wireframe in a few significant ways. Even though the cascade of information is the same, the layout of main elements has changed. This is fine, as I like to think of wireframes as documents that tell us the hierarchy of importance for content and interface elements.

Furthermore, many of you are probably looking at this design and questioning whether it's realistic from a client project perspective. Where is the social integration? Everything seems static. At ten pages, the site is tiny by any standard. Well, yes, all that's true, but consider: everything we've learned that applies to a small site like Spectrumagic also applies to massive sites.

Designing for Interaction

What's nice about this approach is that most of the work for interactions has been done in the Style Tile. We have a couple of attractive styles for buttons, an example of text links, and a play button for multimedia. For most of the buttons and links, I just copied and pasted directly from the Style Tile because it was faster than remaking the same element a number of times.

What you do need to pay attention to is the overall experience provided by the site's interactions. Place related interactive elements near each other. You want the flow from one piece of content to another to feel seamless and simple. For example, if there's an embedded video in the page, its controls should be right next to the video. Similarly, if there's a block of content that acts as a call to action, the related link should be close to the text.

The relationship between content and interaction should be intuitive for the user. That's why embedding text links in a block of text is an excellent way to contextualize the content that the link is connected to. It's hardly scientific; just use common sense. If the link feels unconnected to the content, it probably is.

One way to simplify this problem is to address it in the Style Tile. If you've already designed your buttons and text links in the context of when they'll be used, the problem is already solved. Stick with what works and only deviate from the Style Tile when absolutely necessary.

The Subpage

The subpage, seen in Figure 6.35, shares many of the same design elements as the home page. Clearly, the header is exactly the same (and will be on all the pages), but it does introduce some more patterns that we're yet to review.

The image grid is used to link to related subjects on the site. It's a simple solution, because it's easy to add pages. For example, if I wanted to add five pages to the Color Theory section of our website, I'd just add five images here, and then link them to the new pages of content I'd just created.

Another design element introduced on this page is an `aside`, which is a sidebar of closely related content; it usually takes the form of off-site links, quotes, images, or important information that's distinct from the flow of the main content. An aside is also a good place to put syndicated content such as blog posts, tweets, and RSS feeds.

The last element added with this design is "What the Science?!" at the bottom of the page. Because the site has two main content areas: Color Theory and Optics, each content page uses this section to correlate the two. In this case, "What the Science?!" shows the user what pages in the Optics content are related to Color Theory. We want to encourage users to bounce back and forth between both major content areas, so that they gain a broad understanding of the website subject. Providing embedded links gives them easy access to that content.

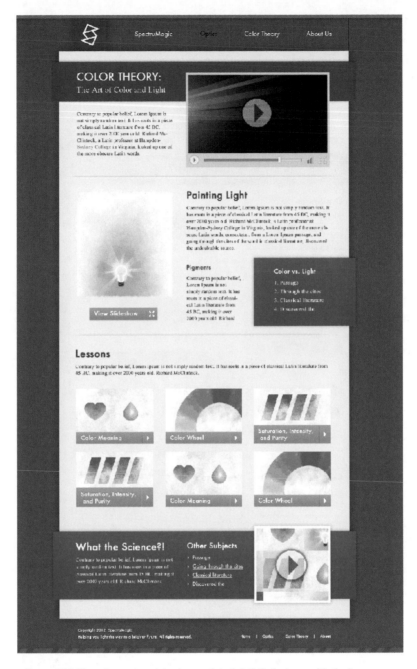

Figure 6.35. The subpage template shares a lot of stylistic features with the home page

Special Pages

In the section called "Overcoming the Problem" in Chapter 4, we talked about what pages you'll need to design to show the client. This will always include a home page and subpage in order to demonstrate how most pages will be used. The subpage is treated like a template where any piece of content can go, and because every project is different, the level of detail will vary. In the case of Spectrumagic, I added a lot of detail for the purposes of demonstrating how it can be used.

Sometimes, you'll have to design additional pages; admin sections, forms, ecommerce areas, or media-specific pages are common examples of pages that require custom design. You can expect to have a number of custom designs, such as the one in Figure 6.36, for every project; only rarely will it be just the home page and one subpage template.

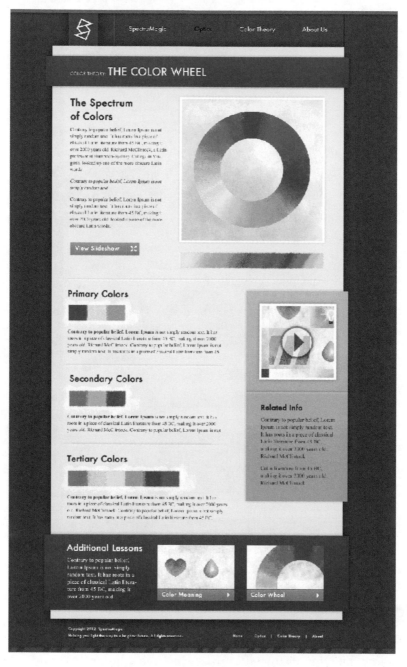

Figure 6.36. A content-heavy special page

For Spectrumagic, I designed a content-heavy page. The color wheel page is a good example of one requiring heavy customization. Because the client requested that the site have lots of interaction and imagery, I chose to display much of the content as images. This page has one subject, which is a good rule of thumb for a content page, and has been custom-arranged so that the connections between each piece of content are obvious. Most of the customization has to do with page layout; this page draws from the same Style Tile as our other two mockups to be visually consistent, even though the layout is completely different.

I wanted to ensure that certain elements were carried over from the other subpage design so that the user is able to find related content easily. The image grid is also on this page, even though it occupies much less screen real estate than it did on the subpage template.

This site will have a number of customized pages, such as the "Color Wheel" page, and each of these pages will have to be laid out to accommodate the content. It's unnecessary to mock up each one in Photoshop for the client beforehand, but you should definitely do one or two so that the client is clear about your intentions.

Intuitive Design

I'm just going to go ahead and say it: there is no cut-and-dried "right" process. These processes have been created to try to structure our work for any number of reasons: streamlining might save time and money, or the design company might have too many people to keep track of all the bits and pieces that make up the project. Without a process and the terminology associated with it, we'd have no way to communicate meaningfully about our work.

When you get down to brass tacks, we're just trying to smooth out a process to avoid it becoming convoluted, too subjective, or painful. I've laid out a number of small processes that work for me and have done so for others. You'll have to decide whether you want to adopt the same course of action.

For instance, let's talk about wireframing. Some folks bypass them. Oh yes, you heard me. They skip that part and move on to thumbnails. But no one is excommunicating them from the profession. I like wireframes because they're a quick way for me to gain a handle on page structure and content hierarchy. I prefer employing them because they abstract all the visual crud that clients can get hung up on.

But that isn't everyone's cup of tea. Meagan Fisher told me that she likes to mark up her wireframes in the browser and treat them like simple versions of the site. She uses the same HTML for her final designs as she does for the wireframes. She even skips traditional PSD mockups, preferring to do that in the browser too. I know, she's a rebel!

Everything I've said up to this point is just my opinion. I encourage you to try everything that you can think of when hammering out a website. I'll always advocate experimentation, so onwards and upwards, kids.

Don't Go Home Just Yet

We've walked through the entire design process from initially talking to a client to setting the project parameters to crafting a set of final mockups. Overall, most measures will achieve the results you want under the right circumstances. We've defined a fairly clear series of steps for gathering data, imagining creative ideas, organizing content, and drafting designs.

But what about monkey wrenches? What about all the unforeseen problems that can hinder a project?

Occasionally, unexpected situations arise, or some of the tweaks you'd like to do to your designs are unfeasible because of certain limitations or circumstances. In the next chapter, we'll talk about some of those limitations and how to adjust to them.

On a brighter note, we'll also talk about some of the advances that can make your game plan easier.

Chapter 7

Designing in the Wild

Understanding the technical limitations of web-based technologies and how to navigate those limitations is an important skill set for implementing a design. Often, a little knowledge ahead of time can help to shape a design and make front-end development easier. It's all about shared knowledge.

 Knowledge Is Power

Having knowledge about what is possible or what is difficult in HTML, CSS, and JavaScript will very likely affect the decisions you make while designing.

Embrace the dynamic qualities of modern websites, because you simply won't have the kind of control that's possible in other fields like print design. It's likely that you won't know what the content will be while you're still building the site.

We're now going to talk about some of those limitations and how you can overcome them.

Get Over the Failings of Technology

Web design is not print design, so you just have to accept that you'll be unable to do everything you want to do. There's no point getting hung up on all the limitations of HTML or browsers. Yes, being unable to use HTML5 extensively in a production environment is a shame, but don't let it hold you back. IE6 is pure nightmare fuel, but you can choose to not support it with some projects; for example, if you know that your users will exclusively be using modern browsers, such as in an office intranet environment.

Embrace all the limitations of the Web and you'll create some amazing sites, all without the headache. If you let yourself become bogged down by all the frustrating elements of our industry, you'll burn out. So, in a word, chill. Take a deep breath and prepare for IE conditional comments in your HTML.

Fonts: A Love-Hate Relationship

Typesetting in web design is more difficult than in print because you have less control. CSS allows you to adjust a font's letterspacing, leading, size, and weight, but you lack the same sort of precision over kerning pairs that you would have in a program like Photoshop or InDesign. When loading web fonts, you're forced to rely on the font itself. You have to choose a font that has good type hinting and kerning to begin with, because you have little command over how the browser renders the font; you're unable make subtle adjustments to overcome the font's shortcomings.

Another limitation of web typography is the inconsistency between browser rendering engines. Some browsers have better font smoothing or anti-aliasing, but each browser renders every font in its own way. Because of that variance, font glyphs can take up slightly different amounts of space in various browsers. So line breaks often happen in between different words in assorted browsers, which can have a significant effect on the height of text blocks and headlines.

There is very little you can do to overcome this "problem," but if you accept it as a reality of the medium, you can start creating flexible designs that respond to the unpredictable qualities of typography in your designs.

Users

Accept that everything you do has a purpose and an audience. Part of your job as a designer is to completely comprehend the purpose so that you can provide end users with what they need. It doesn't matter whether you're building an information-based site or a web app; you have to know your target audience to effectively do your job.

So how do you determine who the end user is?

In the section called "Communicating with Clients" in Chapter 3, we went through a discovery process where we asked the client a series of questions about the business, the product, and its customers. This process is designed to help you understand the end user, because, more often than not, clients know more about their customers than we do.

However, the preliminary questions will only go so far. A website is a living document; it's constantly in flux for good reason. Once a website is built and users start interacting with it, you inevitably start to see patterns in how it's being used, what parts of the site the users are ignoring, and what features users want that are missing. I think of every website's launch date as the beta launch of the website, even if it isn't officially a beta version. Knowing how people use a site requires testing. It's impossible to know what works well until you see people try to use it. Most sites that I build have Google Analytics[1] or another analytics tracking system in use, just so that we can have basic data about what parts of the site are visited and ignored. I've also used services like Crazy Egg[2] to create heat maps and scroll maps.

Handy tools like these provide information that you otherwise would be without. Whenever you design a website, you're forced to make assumptions about what will work, what will look good, and what the user will want to do. You could look at the analytics for websites similar to your own for an idea of what to expect. Still, you can never be 100% certain that your assumptions are correct until you have real data.

Avoid worrying too much about it all; just learn to think of websites as constantly changing, living documents.

Dynamic Content (Should that box really hold 500 words?)

Many websites, especially larger sites, are built with some kind of content management system (CMS). The purpose of a CMS is to allow clients to manage their own websites. They can update page content, create or delete pages, and manage syndicated content like blog posts or calendars. Giving clients this level of control over websites has pros and cons. An upside is that we're saved from spending as much time maintaining existing websites, because the client can handle the menial changes to text or content. The downside of providing clients with a certain level of control is that they might break the website with their changes.

Say you've designed a website with two columns: a main content area that will hold the page content, and a smaller sidebar that holds syndicated content such as blog post titles. You designed the sidebar so that it will comfortably hold five blog post titles of no more than 15 words each; however, the system fails to enforce this limitation. You've even provided the client with a set of written instructions on what's possible (and what's not) with the site.

You have just screwed up in a number of ways. Just for giggles, let's list those ways:

- A content area has been created that's intended for dynamic content that is itself not dynamic.

- You've created a design that displays up to 15 words in each header, but the system allows the client to exceed this limit.

- You've provided written instructions to a client … tsk, tsk.

It's a rookie mistake to force a client into a pattern of behavior. Why should the client be restricted to 15 words in a blog post title? Is it in their best interest? Perhaps, but a client should have control

---

[1] http://www.google.com/analytics/
[2] http://www.crazyegg.com/

over their own content. Luckily, you can make some simple changes to overcome all of these problems.

Enable the client to write a 30-word blog post title if it's been requested. If the page layout requires that the title be less than 15 words, the title can be truncated programmatically in the sidebar and be a link to the blog post containing the full title in the main content area.

An even simpler solution would be to design a sidebar that can accommodate five blog post titles of any length. By letting the sidebar's height remain dynamic, it will expand and contract vertically depending on the content inside.

Finally, if you have to provide the client with a set of instructions for what they can and can't do on the website, the job is probably unfinished. You should address the problems yourself so that the client is saved from dealing with them on a day-to-day basis. This blog post title problem is a good example. You should never give the client an instruction saying that a blog post title cannot be longer than 15 words. Either handle it programmatically, or adjust the design so that it's no longer a limitation. At most, write guidelines for content management within your design, such as at what length you should truncate content, add pagination, or archive the content to another area.

You'll run into problems like this all the time, because it's hard to anticipate everything that will be put on the site or changed once you pass site control to the client. You should think long and hard about the decisions you make to mitigate potential problems in the future; if a client does something crazy with their content and breaks the site, they probably won't take the rap. They're going to blame you, and they'll be right.

Pushing the Medium

We are an industry obsessed with tools. Every web designer I know can wax philosophical on the joys of CSS3 and all modern web technology, but the reality is that many bleeding-edge technologies are poorly supported because so many users have outdated hardware and software. Web browsers like IE 6, 7, and 8 don't support recent additions to CSS like the `box-shadow` or `border-radius` properties. This isn't really a big deal, it just demands a slightly different approach to web design.

First things first … we should talk browsers.

Browsers

We've already touched on this a couple of times, but browsers play a major role in how users experience your website. All browser types support distinct features and function slightly differently; they can have a major impact on your website if these areas of difference are overlooked. Figure 7.1 shows the Google home page in Firefox, Chrome, Safari, and Opera.

Figure 7.1. Modern browsers support a selection of cutting-edge features of CSS and HTML

In my opinion, browsers fall into two categories: modern browsers and legacy browsers. Modern browsers, such as Mobile Safari and Chrome, support many newer features of HTML, CSS, and JavaScript. Legacy browsers are those that have been superseded by newer browsers, and will never be upgraded to support modern features. The most notable legacy browser—at least, the one that causes the most problems—is Internet Explorer 6. It has no support for any of the modern features and has a number of bugs that make laying out pages difficult.

A website should work across several modern and legacy browsers, which means creating code that's sometimes redundant and performing a lot of bug testing. Additionally, there is a growing number of users who are visiting websites on mobile devices, like smartphones and tablets, which have their own browsers as well. Luckily, smartphone and tablet browsers are all modern and updated regularly, but that still leaves us with the issue of old browsers.

That begs the question: what are we supposed to do? The answer is progressive enhancement.

Progressive Enhancement

The concept of progressive enhancement states that one must first design a website that can work and display legibly in every browser. Only then can we add modern design features like rounded corners, box shadows, and text shadows for more advanced browsers. The end result of this is that you have a website that is readable across all browsers, even though it looks slightly different in each. It might have rounded corners in the most recent version of Chrome, but have square corners in IE7. By considering every browser in your design, you avoid a situation where unsupported features are necessary for the design, or the site is rendered impossible to read.

Progressive enhancement helps when designing websites to function in older browsers while giving users a slightly richer experience with newer browsers. Sadly, it's unable to help us overcome all of the variance, because older browsers have bugs. Listing all the bugs that you'll come across while debugging your websites is beyond the scope of this book, but The CSS3 Anthology[3] is worth a read if you want to dig into a little code. In addition to that, you should learn some tools that can help you find, identify, and resolve any issues.

Fancy Tools

As designers and front-end developers, we have quite a few amazing tools at our disposal. We've already talked about a number of them (Balsamiq, Photoshop, and so forth), but I try to avoid emphasizing tools too much. Ultimately, they're just a means to an end. If you design everything with paper and pencil and then go straight to markup with a basic text editor, kudos to you. Any tool set is a good one if the job is done efficiently and quickly.

Still, I have a few tools that are impossible to live without. These apps are simple to employ and very powerful. If you're already using them, this section will be old hat. Otherwise, strap that belt a little tighter, because you'll be adding to it.

Art Apps: Design that Biz

All the cool kids are using Photoshop these days. It's a robust app that allows us to do almost anything we want with images, but it wasn't originally created to be a design app. Over the years, functionality has been added that's made Photoshop standard for many creative industries. Digital artists, web designers, matte painters, print studios, and so on all use Photoshop on a daily basis.

Chances are that even if you have only been designing for a little while, you already have it as part of Adobe's design package. Maybe you were given it as a student or you just bit the bullet and bought it outright (just don't pirate it!). Either way, in no time you'll see that Photoshop is a huge and daunting app with hundreds of fiddly bits. (Check out SitePoint's *Photoshop CS6 Unlocked*[4] for some great info). Luckily, you will rarely need all of Photoshop's functionality to be a web designer.

I use Photoshop every day, so, needless to say, I'm a big fan. Still, I thought I'd list a few other apps that can perform many of the same functions.

Fireworks (http://www.adobe.com/products/fireworks.html)
> Fireworks is another Adobe product that some say is better suited for web design. I hardly ever use this app, but I know it offers a great deal of functionality that's missing from Photoshop.

---

[3] http://www.sitepoint.com/books/cssant4/
[4] http://www.sitepoint.com/books/photoshop2/

For instance, Fireworks allows you to add multiple states (such as "hover") to design elements and then preview them interactively. It also has a system for creating pages and master pages, similar to InDesign. Master pages allow you to design elements that will appear on multiple pages, such as the header or footer. Fireworks is also set up to design numerous pages in one project file, which sounds handy. If you've ever had to design several iterations of Photoshop mockups, you'll appreciate the ability to have assorted designs in one document.

The only reason why I'm not using Fireworks is that everyone I work with uses Photoshop. It's easier to pass around documents and to work on each other's projects if we all work in the same app.

If you have Fireworks and there's no need for you to stick to Photoshop, give it a try.

GIMP (http://www.gimp.org/)

The GNU Image Manipulation Program is basically the poor man's Photoshop, offering much of the same functionality. GIMP is a cross-platform, open-source project that you can download for free. Its interface has been less than pleasing, but the good news is that change is on the cards as I write.[5] The app is certainly usable. I believe you could easily do anything in GIMP that you can do in Photoshop, though opinion is mixed.

The only downside is that very few people seem to use GIMP professionally. Perhaps the indifference stems from the perception that because it's free, it's inferior to Photoshop. Still, if you're a student or freelancer who is unable to drop the cash for Photoshop, GIMP is a viable option.

Sketch 2 (http://www.bohemiancoding.com/sketch/)

Sketch 2 is a newcomer to Apple's App Store. I aimed to keep this book platform-independent, but I really like this app so I've made an exception that Mac users will benefit from.

Sketch 2 is a lightweight app that combines all the features an interface designer will need from Illustrator, Photoshop, and Fireworks. While it has less functionality than any of the three, it does have all the features you'll actually use. It's a nicely designed vector app made specifically for interactive designers, and includes an infinite canvas, multiple (useful) export options, and a slew of other features just for us.

It is still a bit buggy in places, but looks promising. Considering that it can be had for a measly $50, and only takes up around 16MB on your hard drive, Sketch 2 is definitely worth the test drive.

Google It

Seriously, everyone needs to know how to search for information. It's simply impossible to be an expert on all subjects. Even a basic web design has a lot of moving parts, so it's important to be able

---

[5] http://gui.gimp.org/index.php/GIMP_UI_Redesign

to learn new technology and brush up on certain topics. Even the best of us need to do a little research now and again.

Our industry is great at documenting bugs and features, so taking a second to google your problem is likely to yield an answer that you can use immediately. Often, websites or blog posts about a given subject will also contain a wealth of ancillary information, so it's a great way to find this stuff out. Sometimes it's fun to follow through a bunch of links and learn stuff you had no idea about.

Dev Tools

We haven't really talked much about developing websites, but it is important that you take into account how your sites will be marked up and implemented.

The problems created by browser inconsistencies can be hard to overcome, so a good first step is to develop in an environment that allows you to test your code easily. I use a few tools that give me immediate feedback on my HTML, CSS, and JavaScript, as well as letting me see how my designs will render in multiple browsers.

Using browser dev tools definitely takes some adjustment, but after a while it will become second nature. Here are the three main tools I use:

Firebug (http://getfirebug.com/)
> Firebug is a plugin for Firefox that provides a robust developer tool set. The main feature that I use is the Inspector, shown in Figure 7.2, which allows me to view my HTML and CSS in real time, make changes on the fly, and gain additional information about system defaults. If you're writing JavaScript, Firebug comes with a console that shows error information and outputs, and practically anything that you want. It is great for debugging scripts.

> Firebug is a staple of most web designers' development pipeline, and a great tool for any front-end developer. I would recommend giving it a shot.

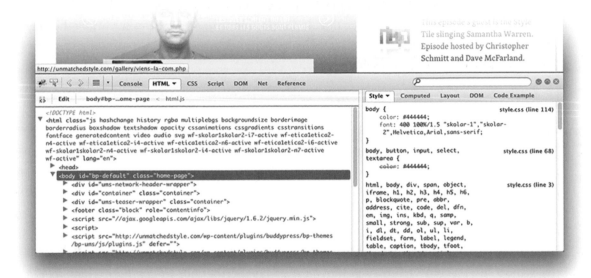

Figure 7.2. Firebug is a web developer's best friend

Chrome Developer Tools

In the last year or so, I've switched from Firebug to Chrome as my main development browser. Chrome also comes with a sound development tool set, very similar to Firebug. It has an Inspector and console that function almost identically to Firebug's, and can be seen in Figure 7.3.

Figure 7.3. Chrome developer tools are my jam right now

Whether you use Chrome or Firebug is really a personal preference. Avoid overthinking it; just pick one that works for you, because developing your site in either browser is just the beginning. Once you have a bug-free, functioning website, you then need to test in as many other browsers as possible.

That's where BrowserStack comes in.

BrowserStack (http://www.browserstack.com/)

BrowserStack is a handy app that tests websites across many browsers on several operating systems. BrowserStack's home page, visible in Figure 7.4, shows some of its best features. If you want to see what your website looks like on Windows XP in IE6, BrowserStack can show you in real time. Unlike many other testing suites that only show you a static image of how your website would look in an older browser, BrowserStack emulates the older browser live so that you're actually interacting with it. You can click links and navigate the website, just like you would in your native browser. It even runs JavaScript code and plugins such as Flash.

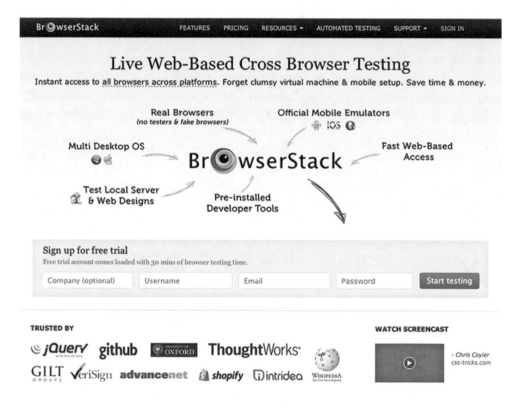

Figure 7.4. BrowserStack lets you test sites and debug

Be aware, however, that BrowserStack's rendering quality is fairly low, the site is slow, and the interface leaves much to be desired. But the functionality it provides far outweighs these shortcomings. After using it on just a few sites, I'm unable to imagine testing without it. With a little luck, some of BrowserStack's issues will be resolved in future updates; but even with its shortcomings, this app is more than worth it.

CSS Tools: Whizbangery

CSS is relatively easy to understand, but there's a lot to remember. Having some handy tools that help you translate your designs into CSS can reduce your front-end dev time and make your life a whole lot easier.

Some of these tools are really progressive and involve an extensive change in your workflow and front-end development pipeline. Others provide a visual way of writing CSS rules, which are by their nature abstract. None of these tools are necessary to be a good designer or front-end developer, but they can simplify how you develop.

CSS3 Generator (http://css3generator.com)

It has to be said: I love this little app. I have a hard time remembering all the syntax for CSS3 properties, but all I have to do is go to CSS3 Generator, tell it what I'm trying to accomplish, and it gives me the CSS I need. Even if you do know the syntax (including all the vendor prefixes), it's often faster to just copy and paste the code than to write it multiple times. There's more than one app out there like this, but I prefer CSS3 Generator because it's fairly comprehensive and intuitive.

Mind you, there are better ways of handling CSS3 properties. If you've heard of Sass or LESS, I'll be doing a quick intro shortly. But if you're wanting to learn all that CSS3 has to offer, or if you need a quick reference for CSS3 properties that you struggle to remember, this is a good site to fall back on.

You might want to also check out CSS3Please[6] or ColorZilla.[7] The nice thing about using these visual tools is that the more you use them, the better you understand CSS3 and eventually you won't need them anymore.

CSS Preprocessors

When writing all the CSS rules required to style your website, you'll often find yourself writing the same code over and over again, or you have to introduce nonsemantic HTML classes to target with your CSS. CSS is also limited in its capabilities, unlike scripting or programming languages, which allow you to use variables and functions, for example. CSS will only let you write selectors and properties.

To overcome CSS's shortcomings, new tools called preprocessors have cropped up in the last few years. LESS[8] and Sass[9] are two very common CSS preprocessors. They provide features that CSS lacks, such as mixins or nesting. After you write your styles in the preprocessor language, the language is compiled by an interpreter, which uses it to write CSS. The resulting

---

[6] http://css3please.com/
[7] https://addons.mozilla.org/en-US/firefox/addon/colorzilla/
[8] http://lesscss.org/
[9] http://sass-lang.com/

CSS has all the same redundancies that your old CSS would, but you don't have to write it. You only have to write the preprocessor rules, which can speed up production time and greatly simplify the time it takes to make changes.

The Reality of Money: The Root of All Compromise

In addition to technology-based limitations, many of the issues you'll deal with as a designer will be about the client or production schedule. The demands placed on you by having to meet particular deadlines, as well as manage the wishes of multiple stakeholders and limits of a finite budget, will also affect any decisions you make and your ability to invest time into a project.

You can go ahead and boil all of that down to one word: money.

Never lose sight of the fact that you are running a business, and that everything you're doing is assisting your client's business. Often, you'll have to scale your ideas to fit what the client can afford. You want the client to have realistic expectations, so it's important that you're honest about budgetary and time constraints.

Let's discuss what to consider when working on a project and how it will impact your decision-making process.

Production Schedules

Production schedules exist for many reasons. You must lay out a plan of action for any project where milestones denote significant markers. The client needs to know where you're at any given time in a project, while the tasks required to complete a project should be assigned to those people who are best qualified to deal with them.

A production schedule outlines all these factors with enough detail for everyone to understand how the project is going to work. It defines expectations, which ensures that all parties have the same expectations.

Because every project is different, it can be hard to write a production schedule. Parts of a project might take much more time than you anticipated, unforeseen issues will arise, and members of the client team can change their mind at any time, which can destroy even the most stringently adhered-to production schedules.

How I've learned to overcome these issues is to think about a production schedule in a slightly different way. This is just my opinion, but the only deadline that really matters in a web design production schedule is the launch date. Every other deadline should be treated as a milestone that does nothing more than document when a particular task has been completed. Instead of creating expectations for the client that a milestone is attached to a particular date, the milestone should be attached to a particular project task, and all dates except for the launch date should be estimates.

Therefore, rather than telling the client that a particular task will be complete by August 1st, I'd tell them that the task would likely be done sometime in August.

Building a website is a process, and in my opinion, it doesn't really matter when project items are completed, as long as the website goes live when the client needs it to. The only caveat to this is ensuring that other contributors to the project—developers, collaborators, marketers, and so on—aren't restricted to performing their part in the process. You need to make certain very early in a relationship with any client that they understand how design and development work.

Goodbye and Good Luck

It's impossible to cover everything you might need to be a great designer who makes a gazillion dollars, but I can tell you that you have it in you to build wonderful sites for your clients.

If I can leave you with one last piece of advice, it's this: Don't worry over the minor details, enjoy yourself, and never stop learning. Go forth and make great things!

Index

Symbols

960-grid system, 23

A

abduzeedo.com, 66

"above the fold", 75

accents (color), 61

achromatic palettes, 61

Adobe Swatch Exchange (.ase) files, 60, 61

aesthetics, 2

analytics, 154–155

architectural patterns, 106–109

Art Deco, 35

art direction

    about, 140–141

    concept-based, 122–124

    content-based, 141–142

    mood boards, 142–143

    reference material for, 142

    Style Tiles, 143–145

art movements

    Art Deco, 35

    Art Nouveau, 35

    Arts and Crafts movement, 34–35

    Cubism, 40–42

    Geometric Abstraction, 37

    Minimalism, 35–38, 40

    Modernism, 38–40

    Postmodernism, 40–42

Art Nouveau, 35

art tools

    Fireworks, 158–159

    GIMP, 159

    Photoshop, 68, 127, 158

    Sketch 2, 159

Arts and Crafts movement, 34–35

.ase (Adobe Swatch Exchange) files, 60, 61

aside element, 148

audience (*see* users)

B

Balsamiq, 78, 137

Barry, Jay, 137

Bauhaus, 39

beauty

    defined, 3–4

    design process, 6–9

    of mathematics, 11–12

    perceived, 9–11

    prettiness vs., 8

    relevance of, 9

    subjective nature of, 5–6

Bootstrap, 112

brainstorming, 17

brand colors, 60–61, 62

breakpoints, 90, 130–131, 133–134

browser dev tools, 160–162

browser limitations, 153–154, 156–158

BrowserStack, 162

Burka, Daniel, 12, 53, 80, 127, 128

buttons, vs. links, 112

C

cascading lists, 101

chair arrangements, 21–23

Chrome Developer Tools, 161–162

circular images, 114, 115

"clean" design, 37

client presentations

    games, 56–57

    mood boards, 61–63, 142

    page mockups, 149–151

    past projects, 56

    posters, 56

    storyboards, 63–65

Hey...

Thanks for buying this book. We really appreciate your support!

We'd like to think that you're now a "Friend of SitePoint", and as such would like to invite you to our special "Friends of SitePoint" page.

Here you can SAVE up to 43% on a range of other super cool SitePoint products.

Save up to 43% with this link:

Link: 🌐 sitepoint.com/friends

Password: friends